RAY
TOMA
801-1652

LEE AND HIS CAUSE
The Why and the How of the War Between the States

by
John Richard Deering. D.D.

Chaplain Kentucky Division, U.C.V., Once of Claiborne
Guards, Co. K. 12th Regt. Miss. Vol. Inft., Army Northern
Virginia, and Later of Capt. Quirk's Scouts, Morgan's
Kentucky Cavalry

Ego, verum amo, verum volo mihi dici:
Mendacem odi!—Plautus

THE CONFEDERATE
REPRINT COMPANY
☆　☆　☆　☆
WWW.CONFEDERATEREPRINT.COM

Lee and His Cause
The Why and the How of the War Between the States
by John Richard Deering, D.D.

Originally Published in 1907
by The Neale Publishing Company
New York and Washington

Reprint Edition © 2016
The Confederate Reprint Company
Post Office Box 2027
Toccoa, Georgia 30577
www.confederatereprint.com

Cover and Interior Design by
Magnolia Graphic Design
www.magnoliagrapicdesign.com

ISBN-13: 978-0692651063
ISBN-10: 0692651063

DEDICATION
☆ ☆ ☆ ☆

To My Three Daughters and Six Sons

Who have been faithfully taught the Truth of History, the Nature of our Government, and the Love of our Country; in whom I trust to transmit these precious things to coming generations, as they may have the power, for their own sake, and for the honor of those, who at home, in council chambers, legislative halls, hospital wards, prison cells and on hard-fought fields, have taught and toiled, sorrowed and suffered, bled and died, to maintain and establish them.

CONTENTS

☆ ☆ ☆ ☆

INTRODUCTION

The matter here presented to the reader was first given as a "Memorial Day" Address, before Confederate Veteran Camps, and Chapters of the Daughters of the Confederacy, in several cities and towns. Its original use has modified its final form; whilst to embody more of historic fact, and so enhance the permanent value, its limits have been largely expanded.

There are many and worthy "Lives of Lee," and some excellent "Histories of the United States," and still more abundant "Sketches of Battles and Minor Engagements," with almost innumerable "Narratives of Generals," and of "Commands and Campaigns." Many of these are large and expensive, too heavy for handling and too costly for wide circulation, and their readers are correspondingly few and well to do. This is quite unlike any of those. We have also able and elaborate discussions of the Federal Constitution, with their ample deductions learnedly and long drawn out; but little read and less understood. This is not at all like those. It is as simple, I hope, as short, and makes for truth as much as it lacks of beauty.

We have many other books – some of them, like

the down-easter's razors, *"made to sell,"* and therefore
to suit all sorts of readers all the world over. I am not
concerned that this little book shall please everybody. It
was made to vindicate but one side. The only important
question is, Does it do so? My ambition is to state facts,
not to get money. I cheerfully leave conclusions to my
readers. They may strike, if they will but hear me!

The historical items recorded here are more or
less involved in the solution of questions which have
arisen as to the rightfulness of secession; the origin and
conduct of its cause; the character, motives and
sentiments of the people who espoused and defended it,
as well as of those who forced them to fields of blood. I
thought to give these facts in form so cheap, and style so
terse, as to bring them within the means and times of our
busy men and women. I have tried to condense and yet
comprehend; to be clear, yet not "too dear" for the common people's purse.

"History, as written, if accepted in future years,
will consign the South to infamy," says Honorable J.L.
M. Curry. The truth, the only antidote for the poison of
falsehood, should be set to work at once, or the evil effects will become incurable. No time is to be lost. Soon
the cemetery will hold us all. What shall be then thought
of our cause and conduct will depend upon what we leave
in the books of our era. Books live on. They should not
misrepresent us or our dead. But think of the stream
pouring from the press, a stream so strong and so full of
ignorance of us, and of prejudice against us – think of the
political interests, and sectional rivalries, and financial
superiority, and numerical preponderance, and commercial advantages, and the immense Governmental influence, all combined upon the successful side – will poster-

ity ever know who we were, or why we fought? It all depends upon what they read. This book is a soldier's small contribution of something reliable and readable.

It may not be quite needless to say in this place (though I certainly came near forgetting to say it), that the sentiments expressed in this book or justly inferable from it, are such as befit a Confederate soldier's discussion of war times and topics, and might not have been denied or dissembled without the guilt of insincerity or hypocrisy – qualities hated of God and man.

To have given for every statement my authority, and credit for every fact related, to every author consulted, would have made very unsightly pages, and diverted at most interesting moments, the reader's attention. Due acknowledgment is made in another place in a printed list of "sources," and also by the frequent use of quotation marks throughout the text.

I wish to close this prefatory note without other remark, save a saying that I judge worthy in itself, and well suited to my work, from the pen of Rev. Thomas E. Bond, M.D., of Baltimore.

Truth for her own sake – without calculation of probabilities, or hope of results; Truth, solitary, friendless, impotent, on her way out of the world; Truth at the bar of Pilate, dead on the Cross, still in the grave – Truth, always and everywhere, is the one thing to be sought and kept, defended and clung to. Whenever you see a lie rampant, hit it; wherever a truth down, give a hand to it. There is no nobler work in this life than to help the TRUTH.

JNO. R. DEERING.
October 4th, 1907.
"Dixie," Lexington, Kentucky.

CHAPTER ONE
A Confederate Memorial Address

I believe that, in the end, Truth will conquer
– Wyclif.

Daughters of the Confederacy, Soldiers, Sailors, and Fellow-Citizens:

It is strange to me that I am here to speak to you of Lee and his Cause – the long-lost Cause. A still stranger thing is that you are here to listen to me. My limitations are so limitless! My disabilities are so distressing! As I am a poor preacher, I must of course eschew politics; and I must steer clear of all constitutional questions, for I never studied law or meddled with statecraft; and no matter what was the Constitution, the Amendments 13, 14 and 15, have come to pass and are in force. Why talk about the one, when the others "are it"? (I might reply, simply to know the facts.) Nor dare I mention military matters, for I am unlearned in the science of war, and never practiced the art save as a boy-private on the "far-flung battle line." The field of history is posted against me, so they say, because it has yet to be written. There is no history of the war, for it must be writ-

ten by men unborn, because they weren't in it and know
by experience nothing of it! Our schools are now being
filled with histories, so called, yet the men who helped to
make history must not dare to write it.

The biographical region is also yet closed, because
it is confidently claimed that, we stand too close, we lack
the perspective, which posterity will have, of course, in
which to view the mighty men of renown, as they should
be seen. Just why a man who wasn't born for a century
after Lee had gone to God, will be able to see and know
and describe him better than the one who camped,
marched and fought under him, does not yet appear to
me; but I believe it, of course, because I see it so often in
the newspapers! In sheer despair, I thought of Lee himself
– it is his birthday, and was his cause, as much as ours –
might I not venture to speak of him, but one of our chief
captains? Could I not be cautiously critical, or critically
cautious, modest and moderate, in this solitary instance,
and for a single hour, whilst I should speak of him? Why,
yes, but alas for me! "Only an Apelles may paint Alexander;" – and had I the skill to do it, where is the time for
the task? It would take a year to do the work, and a week
to examine and enjoy it, not an hour. Listen, it has already
been done. Buy for your winter nights, for your college
and city libraries, such volumes as *General Lee*, by
Fitzhugh Lee, his nephew and cavalry commander, and
Robert E. Lee and the Southern Confederacy, by Alexander White, M.A., D.D., Ph.D., and *Personal Reminiscences of General Lee*, by J. William Jones, D.D., his
chaplain in camp and in college; and *Recollections and
Letters of Lee*, by his son Robert, and *Four Years Under
Marse Robert*, by Major Robert Stiles. In these you will
find worthy work from able hands and from ample, origi-

nal sources, work that has already won world-wide fame, and recognition of Lee as the greatest captain of this country, or era, the idol of his army, and as President Davis well said, "The high model for the imitation of generations yet unborn."

The Virginia Lees were of early English stock. R. E. Lee was born January 19th, 1807, in Stratford, Westmoreland County. His father was "Light Horse Harry," Washington's Chief of Cavalry. His mother was Anne Hill Carter. His father dying when he was but eleven, Robert was her very own. When he left home for the academy, she said of him, "Oh, how can I live without Robert, he is both son and daughter to me?" He grew up in Alexandria and went from there at eighteen to West Point, in 1825. In a class of forty-six, he graduated second, in 1829, and without a single mark of demerit. The young lieutenant was married, June 30th, 1831, at Arlington, to the beautiful and charming Mary Randolph Custis, great-granddaughter of Mrs. George Washington. He was then twenty-four, past. Five years later, he was in Mexico under General Winfield Scott, who said, "My success was largely due to the skill, valor and undaunted courage of Captain R. E. Lee." Later, General Scott declared, "Lee is the greatest military genius of America, and the best soldier that I ever saw in the field." He also said that, "If opportunity offers, he will show himself the foremost captain of his time." It isn't at all strange, therefore, that Mr. Lincoln, moved by the old commander's judgment, should have sent Lee, a dozen years later, and when he wanted the best man among men, through Mr. Francis P. Blair, an offer of the command of all the United States forces being organized for the invasion of Virginia; nor that General Scott considered him as worth to the Union cause an army of fifty thousand men; nor can any man wonder that a few days after, Virginia, his noble mother, put into his hands her sword and gave him command of all her troops.

As he stood in her Convention to accept this trust, he was thus described: – "Tall, straight, strong, brown-eyed, of gentle and benevolent countenance, and of remarkable beauty, of unaffected dignity and gravity. In robust health, and of almost boundless powers of endurance, a perfect and beautiful model of manhood." Ladies, I am no artist, but I may hold up a sketch that is as lifelike as it is elegant. I do it with pleasure, for you will enjoy it immensely. It is by the Honorable Ben Hill of Georgia: –

> Lee possessed every trait of other great commanders without their vices. He was a foe without hate, a friend without treachery, a soldier without cruelty and a victim without murmuring. He was a public officer without vices, a private citizen without wrong, a neighbor without reproach, a Christian without hypocrisy, and a man without guilt. He was Cæsar without his ambition, Frederick without his tyranny. Napoleon without his selfishness, Washington without his reward. He was as obedient to authority as a servant, and a royal in authority as a king. He was as gentle as a woman in life, pure and modest as a virgin in thought, watchful as a Roman vestal, submissive to law as Socrates, and grand in battle as Achilles!

Such was our hero – "great in his goodness, and good in his greatness," far beyond his fellows. A careful writer says: – "Such a character for balance, for charity, for affection, for gentleness, for sufficiency, for restraint, for silence, for simple piety, for unconscious greatness, this world has seldom seen."

Mr. W.W. Corcoran, of Washington, a name honored, and revered wherever big-hearted benevolence and the graces of the Christian religion are recognized, was invited by the Committee in charge of the laying of the cornerstone of the Lee monument in Richmond to be present on that occasion. The venerable philanthropist, finding that he could not accept, wrote the letter quoted below in which he thus advisedly speaks of General Lee:

It was my good fortune to have been honored with the immediate acquaintance and close friendship of General Lee during the whole period of his public career; and whether I recall him as he moved in the social sphere, which he adorned by his virtues and graces, or as he towered above his contemporaries on that higher stage where the luster of his great qualities shone in the eyes of the whole civilized world, I can truly say, with no small experience of my fellow-men, that of all the men I ever knew, he always seemed to me the most remarkable for the grandeur as well as for the symmetry of the elements which composed the strength and beauty of his peerless character. For such was the natural constitution and such the harmonious blending of these elements that, in the gentleness and benignity of his demeanor, he was seen to be as great in his goodness as he was good in his greatness.

Like all truly great and good men, General Lee had in the highest degree that simplicity of character which springs from purity of heart as well as from the perfect transparency of a clear intelligence. Endowed with an understanding which was as calm as it was penetrating and profound, he always possessed his soul in a patience which never murmured, and a serenity which was never ruffled, whatever might be the duties he was summoned to perform, or whatever might be the perils he was called to face.

No duty ever found him unprepared. No trial ever shook his steadfast mind. Intrepid in all assaults of fortune, and the very soul of honor, he was the Chevalier Bayard of his day – a knight without fear and without reproach, because in him all that was soldierly in conduct met and mingled with all that was blameless in life. With an integrity which rooted itself in the very fibre of his moral constitution, and which, therefore, never gathered spot nor stain throughout the whole of his long and eventful career, he yet had not the slightest trace of censoriousness in his nature, but walked before men with the modesty and humility born of a deep religious spirit.

It is only those who knew him well in all the serene depths of his mental and moral being, who can account for the heroism he displayed after he had sheathed his sword and bowed, without repining, to the decree of an overruling Providence.

Although the life and example of such a man may justly seem to belong, in some special sense, to the State and section which stood in the clearest sight of all his greatness and all his goodness, yet the whole country may rightly claim its share in the heritage of that renown which all generous minds are quick to accord to exalted virtues wherever found, and to magnanimity of soul wherever it is inspired by a conscientious sense of right.

President Roosevelt, in his life of Thomas H. Benton, says: –

The world has never seen better soldiers than those who followed Lee, and their leader will undoubtedly rank as without exception the very greatest of all the great captains that the English-speaking people have ever brought forth; and this, although the last chief of his antagonists may himself claim to stand as the full equal of Marlborough and Wellington.

Lord Garnet Wolseley, Commander in Chief of the Armies of Great Britain, has said:

> I have met with many of the great men of my time, but Lee alone impressed me with the feeling that I was in the presence of a man who was cast in a grander mold, and made of metal different from, and finer than, that of all other men. I believe that all will admit that Lee towered far above all men on either side in that struggle. I believe Lee will be regarded not only as the most prominent figure of the Confederacy, but as the greatest American of the nineteenth century; whose statue is well worthy to stand on an equal pedestal with that of Washington, and whose memory is equally worthy to be enshrined in the hearts of his countrymen.

Assuming that it takes a great soldier to pronounce a sound judgement upon a soldier's greatness, I beg leave to close this series of tributes with that of the first Lieutenant-General in the Confederate Armies – the man most nearly Lee's equal in military genius, in Christian completeness, and in the admiration and affection of the Southern people. He said, "General Lee is a phenomenon. He is the only man I would be willing to follow blindfold." Such was the estimate of the man whom the world calls "Stonewall Jackson." If the cold mute marble of Lee's tomb shall ever "speak his matchless worth," then the lines inscribed over the dead body of England's mighty and illustrious Christian soldier, Major-General Charles George Gordon, who lies in London's great cathedral, would sum up as truly and express as tersely the virtues of the noblest of all Americans – of our peerless Lee – "who at all times and everywhere gave his strength to the weak, his substance to the poor, his sympathy to the suffering, and his heart to God."

At least three decisions of General Lee and their consequent events in his life were so important, and so illustrative of his character, that they must be recalled here in closing this imperfect account. These were the surrender of his army; the choice of the presidency of Washington College; and his dying without saying a word or leaving a line to vindicate his conduct or enhance his fame.

Whilst moving his army and trains towards Appomattox, the situation (for which Lee was in no wise responsible, because he would, if allowed, have chosen a better line of defense, months before he was forced to leave Petersburg and give up Richmond) became so nearly hopeless through hunger, weakness, marching, fighting, wounds, captures, desertions and the death of brave men, steadfast to the end, that a desperate attack in the early morning of April 9th was ordered upon Grant's surrounding hosts, in strength, "five times our numbers." Col. C.S. Venable, at the General's request, rode to the front at three o'clock that morning to ask General Gordon if he could cut his way through the enemy. He found Gordon with the Chief of Cavalry, Fitzhugh Lee, planning the movement. In reply to the Commander's inquiry, Gordon said: "Tell General Lee I have fought my corps to a frazzle, and I fear I can do nothing unless I am heavily supported by Longstreet's corps." The last attack by Gordon's men had routed Sheridan's cavalry and brought in prisoners and captured cannon, but it also uncovered heavy lines of infantry beyond. When Gordon's reply was borne back to Lee, he said, "Then there is nothing left me but to go and see General Grant, and I would rather die a thousand deaths." A heart-broken subaltern standing near cried, "O General, what will History say of the surrender of the army in the field?" Lee replied, "Yes, I know they will say hard things of us; they will not understand how we were overwhelmed by numbers; but that is not the question. Colonel; the question is, *Is it right to surrender this army?* If it is right, then *I* will take *all* the responsibility."

For General Lee to know his duty was to do it. At Appomattox, he saw it clearly and did it promptly. What it cost him to hand over to his enemy "that body of incomparable infantry, the Army of Northern Virginia," that ragged, half-starved, fighting remnant, no words can tell, unless it may be summed up in these two – *his life!* General Gordon, in a deliberate, carefully prepared address delivered at Richmond soon after Lee's death, said: "Can I ever forget? No, never, never, can I forget the words which fell from his lips as I rode beside him amid the dejected and weeping soldiers, when turning to me, he said, 'I could wish that I were numbered among the fallen in the last battle.'"

The soldier's death would have been the easy, the glorious thing. Lee craved it, and spoke of it, but was too great and good to court it. He chose the harder lot of living and working, suffering and sorrowing over his vanquished people and ruined country. During the agonizing hours of suspense and whilst he was weighing the momentous interests and obligations involved in the question of longer resistance – burdened with the trust laid upon him, and bending under the weight of woe about to fall upon his beloved Southland – he exclaimed from the depth of his tender heart, – so one of his officers tells us, – "How easily I could get rid of this and be at rest! I have only to ride along the lines and all will be over! But, *it is our duty to live* – for what will become of the women and children of the South, if we are not here to support and protect them?" Fortunately, our splendid leader had the strength to do this; and for five and a half years did it.

The one thing that he was determined to die rather than do, was not so much as named to him. General J. A. Early declares that, in his last conversation with Lee, when the surrender was mentioned, Lee told him that he "had only 7,900 men with arms in their hands, but that when he went to meet General Grant, he left orders with Gordon and Longstreet to hold themselves in readiness, and that he had determined to cut his way out at all hazards, if such terms were not granted as he thought his army was entitled to demand." General Lee had feared to suggest to Grant any willingness to listen to terms, lest Grant should suspect his weakness and ask "an unconditional surrender," and "sooner than that, I am resolved to die," so reads the record made by General Fitzhugh Lee. General Grant perhaps knew the Confederate Chieftain too well to mention any "terms inconsistent with the honor of my army." So far from it, he requested General Lee to state what he regarded as honorable terms, and when it had been done, Grant assented and wrote them, at Lee's request, and then both captains signed them, and Lee and his aide, Colonel Marshall, rode off, prisoners on parole. He had calmly taken "all the responsibility." Forty-two years have rolled away, and with them soldiers, great and small, but till now, no voice has been heard in condemnation of the men or his deed.

With the close of his career as Commander of the Confederate Armies, there came to General Lee the question of future employment. Many business interests sought his services. Among these, a corporation in Atlanta made him an offer with very fine salary. A wealthy insurance company would have given many thousands for the mere use of his name. His preference, as expressed in a letter to a friend, was a "little quiet house in the woods, where I can procure shelter and my daily bread, if permitted by the victor. I wish to get Mrs. Lee out of the city as soon as practicable." The curiosity of crowds and homage of admirers was more than they could bear.

Very lucrative business proposals were kindly declined. To one such, his reply was: "I am grateful, but I have a self-imposed task which I must accomplish. I have led the young men of the South in battle; I have seen many of them die on the field; I shall devote my remaining energies to training young men to do their duty in life."

The presidency of more than one university was declined for some one or another reason. On August 5, 1865, he was lovingly urged to accept the headship of "Washington College of Virginia." There was in the offer, says Professor E. S. Joynes, who knew it best, "absolutely nothing that could have tempted him." His habits, associations, pecuniary interests and strong desires for privacy and quietude were all against it. The school had merely local reputation and patronage. The salary was only $1,500; hardly half a living for those cruel times. The college buildings, apparatus, libraries, and investments were all wrecked by the waves of war. Nor had it credit, patronage, or prospects to speak of. The faculty of four had been only partially paid and the students numbered but forty. There was also considerable debt. Our land was wasted, our people crushed, our hopes buried. Everywhere the struggle was for food and fire and shelter; not for the arts or sciences or literature. The position could confer neither fame nor fortune. Its acceptance by General Lee was due, says Professor Joynes, "to a profound and deliberate sense of duty." Why! the man who carried him the official notification of his election to the presidency had to borrow the money for his journey's expense, and also the suit of clothes that he wore, and which had been recently sent to his friend by a son sojourning in New York, in order to appear decently garbed before the greatest of Virginians. The bearer of the honor to be bestowed upon Lee was the Hon. John W. Brockenbrough, Rector of the college, and thus was obtained his outfit for the mission.

General Washington had in 1785, accepted from the State of Virginia $50,000, as a gift in appreciation of his very successful services to the Commonwealth and the Union, upon condition that he might use it "for the education of the children of the poor, particularly of such as had fallen in defense of their country." This sum he had donated to the school then known as "Liberty Hall Academy," and thenceforward by his own honored name. The friends of General Lee believe that his desires so far coincided with this deed and desire of Washington as to have determined him in the devotion of his remaining years to the same noble end. To him it seemed, says Bishop Wilmer "the door of Providence." It was the opportunity to do somewhat by way of compensation to Virginia for the loss of her wealth, strength and manhood. He seized and used it. The Trustees, who having neither silver nor gold, had the wisdom and "happy audacity" to choose Lee for their College's Head Master, made no mistake. So correct was their knowledge of his character, and so well-founded their faith in his impoverished countrymen, that all the rest worked out rightly. They gave Lee work and bread, and he brought to their College, honor, patronage, and immortality.

If any doubt could have arisen as to the motives of the Christian soldier in taking the President's place, or as to his fitness for it, it must have been dispelled by his own remark to Dr. W. S. White: "I shall be disappointed, sir, I shall fail in the leading object that brought me here, unless these young men all become consistent Christians." Again, he said, – "I dread the thought of any student's going away from the College without becoming a sincere Christian." And he was not denied the desire of his heart in seeing the salvation of "many of the young men of the South."

General Lee left nothing in the way of vindication of his choice or career. Conscious of his rectitude, he was unconcerned for his fame. Till his death, he was silent, though often urged to write. For a time, he did think of a narrative of his campaigns, and made a slight effort to collect materials for it, but being denied all use of the records in Government custody, and the destruction in the retreat of his own personal papers still further preventing him, the thought was given up. Nor was it ever in his mind to publish anything to justify himself. In requesting from one of his generals a report, he plainly tells him – "I shall write this history not to vindicate myself, or promote my own reputation. I want that the world shall know what my poor boys, with their small numbers and scant resources, succeeded in accomplishing." To another, he wrote – "My only object is to transmit the truth to posterity and to do justice to our brave soldiers." And more than anything else, let it be ever remembered, that the fear of bringing blame upon some whose failure to obey orders had been most disastrous to our cause prevented Lee from writing in honor of the men whose devotion, gallantry, endurance and achievement have become the wonder of the world.

An extract from a letter written to General J. A. Early in Mexico, March 15, 1866, shows clearly how very reluctant he was to speak or write, even in his own defense. He refers first to attacks being then made upon President Davis, and later says – "The accusations against myself I have not thought proper to notice, or even to correct misrepresentations of my words and acts. We shall have to be patient, and suffer for a while at least; and all controversy, I think, will only serve to prolong angry and bitter feelings, and postpone the period when reason and charity may resume their sway."

A month later, to another friend, he writes; –

Your letter of the 5th inst., inclosing a slip from the *Baltimore American,* has been received. The same statement has been published at the North for several years. The statement is not true, but I have not thought proper to publish a contradiction; . . . believing that those who know me would not credit it, and those who do not would care nothing about it. I cannot now depart from the rule I have followed. It is so easy to make accusations against the people at the South upon similar testimony, that those so disposed, should one be refuted, will immediately create another; and thus you would be led into endless controversy. I think it is better to leave their correction to the return of reason and good feeling. Thanking you for your interest in my behalf, and begging you to consider my letter as intended only for yourself, I am, most respectfully, your obedient servant, R. E. Lee.

There is scarce an end to such expressions of repugnance to speak upon the platform or write for the press, either in behalf of himself or in defense of his people. He longed for peace and good will, regardless of reputation, past, present or to come, and hence could not be moved by love or lucre to break his self-imposed silence. Thus he lived and died, the unpardoned patriot, the paroled prisoner, the citizen without a country, or the right to vote in the State which his fathers and he had fought to liberate, establish, enlarge and ennoble. Two of his utterances can never be forgotten; "I determined at the outset of her difficulties to share the fate of my people." Once in replying to Hon. Robert Ould's letter proposing to him to accept the nomination for the Governorship of Virginia, in deference to the wishes of the leading men of the Commonwealth, Lee concludes his refusal of the honor in this language; – "If my disfranchisement and privation of civil rights would secure to the citizens of the State the enjoyment of civil liberty and equal rights under the Constitution, I would willingly accept them in their stead." How noble! How like the magnanimous Soul, who riding about on the bloody field of Gettysburg to rally his retreating troops after that murderous repulse, for which certain subordinate commanders were alone to blame, said so cheerfully – *Never mind, men; all this has been my fault.* It is I that have lost this fight, and you must help me out of it, the best way you can." Was ever nobility so noble?

In sheer despair, my comrades, I leave Lee for your leisure, and to your library, whilst I turn to topics which have not been so often presented, or so eloquently depicted – to the cause and consequent war, matters so much misunderstood; so often misrepresented.

CHAPTER TWO:
That Conflict Was Plainly a People's War
☆ ☆ ☆ ☆

My Country; may she be always in the right; but right or wrong, my Country – Commodore Stephen Decatur

The whole heart of Dixie was in it. As a people the South deeply deplored, but bravely accepted it, and fought it through to the end, the bitter end. Not all were secessionists, but the majority were, and the rest rapidly became so. Not all believed in slavery, but the masses did. The Union had no truer friend than Lee himself, who said, "I think slavery a greater evil to the white than to the black race." And his State had opposed it even in her Colonial days. Lee had declared, "If the millions of slaves in the South were mine, I would free them with a stroke of the pen, to avert this war." Thomas Jefferson, the expounder of States' Rights and the founder of Democracy, had been "The consistent enemy of every form of slavery." Patrick Henry once said – "Much as I deplore slavery, I see that prudence forbids its abolition." And Virginia, the proud mother of these patriots, was the first of all the American commonwealths to outlaw the slave trade. Secession also was firmly opposed by many who later died for Dixie under the Stars and Bars; but the war was something different; it was forced upon us, and it was for political self-preservation, – "For God, and Home, and native Land!" The *war* was for the very existence of sovereign States, for "life, liberty and the pursuit of happiness," – not to break up the Union. We had nothing against the Union, but very much against the party which was running the Federal Government, and it was only when all hope of bringing it – *viz.* the Abolition majority – to respect the Constitution and laws of the Union had died in loyal breasts, only then, that ordinances of secession were passed, and the "Solid South" began to be. There was in Southern hearts no lack of loyalty to the General Government: the trouble was the sad want of loyalty on the part of the Government to the local welfare and political rights of the Southern people. According to Mr. R. E. Lee, Jr., the withdrawal of the States grew out of *that.*

A more intelligent and truthful witness living or dead could not be found to testify upon this subject than Bishop George F. Pierce, nor did any such witness ever speak more eloquently in defense of his people than did he in his "Fast Day Sermon, delivered before the General Assembly of Georgia, in the city of Millidgeville, on March 27th, 1863," in which I find the following undeniable statement: –

This war is not of our seeking. We labored to avoid it. Our propositions for amicable adjustment were rejected with subtlety and guile. We claimed only our own. We asked nothing of our enemies. We do not seek their land, or houses, or property. We are not fighting to extend our territory, to subdue a neighboring people, to usurp dominion, to gratify ambition, or malice, or revenge. Faithful to the letter and the spirit of the old Constitution – asserting only the fundamental right of self-government, we are but defending ourselves against a proud, rapacious, malignant foe, who, without right or reason, against law and right and humanity, comes down full of hate and rage to enslave or exterminate us. We are fighting for liberty and home and family; for firesides and fields and altars; for all that is dear to the brave, or precious to the good; for our herds and our flocks, our men servants and maid servants; for the heritage of our fathers and the rights of our children; for the honor of humanity and the institutions of Providence. We are fighting against robbery and lust and rapine; against ruthless invasion, a treacherous despotism, the blight of its own land, and the scorn of the world; mongrel armies whose bond of union is plunder, and whose watch-words are but delusion and falsehood; a fraud upon the African, a lie to the North, and an insult to the South. There is therefore no object proposed by our Government, no end aimed at on which we may not consistently, piously, Scripturally invoke the Divine blessing. We may pray "according to the will of God." The triumph of our arms is the triumph of right and truth and justice. The defeat of our enemies is the defeat of wrong and malice and outrage. Our Confederacy has committed herself to no iniquitous policy, no unholy alliances, no unwarrantable plans either for defense or retaliation, and *now,* with numerous hostile hosts quartered on her soil, and a powerful navy beleaguering her coast, amid provocations innumerable, under threatenings the most diabolical, without fear of the future, ready for the conflict if our deluded, infatuated enemies urge it on her, she is ready to make peace on just and honorable terms. In praying for such a government, I feel that the way to the mercy seat is open. My faith is unembarrassed. My hope is buoyant. I feel that I have access to Him who rules in righteousness. The attitude of our country is sublime. With her foot planted on right and her trust in God, undismayed by numbers and armaments and navies, without the sympathy of the world, shut in, cut off, alone, she has battled through two long, weary years, gallantly, heroically, triumphantly, and to-day is stronger in men, resources, faith and hope than when Fort Sumter's proud flag was lowered to her maiden arms. It is the Lord's doing, and it is marvelous in our eyes. Standing, then, upon the justice of our cause and the righteousness of our aim, and encouraged by the experience of the past, let us lift up humble, thankful hearts to the God of all our mercies, and with emboldened faith commit our destiny into His hand, whom winds and seas obey, who ruleth in the armies of heaven and among the inhabitants of earth.

The ordinances of secession were acts of the people's representatives, and so, of the people themselves; not of the politicians, as we are now told, on every side. Hear one speak who has the best right to testify. When Mr. Lincoln made the call for troops to invade the South, the President of the Virginia Convention, Mr. J. B. Baldwin, who had himself voted against secession, said – "There are now no Union man in Virginia; but those who were Union men will stand to their arms, and make a fight which shall go down in history as an illustration of what a brave people will do in defense of their liberties, after having exhausted every means of pacification."

Was this not a true prophet? And his statement concerning Virginia applies as well to the other Southern States. There were many Unionists among the ignorant and illiterate mountaineers of Eastern Kentucky and Tennessee and Western Virginia, but the South was practically solid for secession after Lincoln's call for troops to subdue her. General Lee was himself a leader, social, civil, and military, yet even he was not needed to lead the secession movement. He was rather a reluctant and unwilling witness of it. He thought it a calamity. Whilst it was going forward, he wrote on January 23d, 1861, "I must try and be patient and await the end, for I can do nothing to hasten or retard it." I do not deny that political doctrine had political expounders, nor that they did a deal of talking, but the people, as free citizens, did both the voting and the fighting. They had to, and so the war became their own; it absorbed them; in it the sun rose and set; to it, they gave their time, money, energy, heads, hearts, fortunes, families and sacred honor; for it everything gave way, at home and abroad, public and private, civil and social, educational and religious, domestic and governmental. It was soon the theme of shop and street, of fireside and counting-room, of barn and business house; it filled our papers, letters, songs, sermons, prayers, table-talk and telegrams; it speedily closed out our schools and colleges, shut up stores, banks, places of amusement, resorts of pleasure and health, and even houses of worship; it opened mines for lead, copper and saltpetre, mills for cotton-thread, for domestic yarns, for high explosives, for percussion caps, for rifles, bayonets, saddles and sabers. The business of turning out blankets, clothes, shoes, hats, canteens, cartridge boxes and cooking utensils, was booming from Texas to old Virginia. Magazines, hospitals, bureaus of information, depots of supplies sprang up as by magic. Then appeared those domestic legions, that no man could number, of wool-carders, yarn-spinners, sock-knitters, weavers of cloths, the gray, and the brown, and the mixed, like Joseph's coat; but what were these compared with the glove-makers, the hat and helmet braiders, button-cutters, belt, buckle, and sword-knot contrivers; or these compared to the braiders of gold lace, weavers of rye straw, and makers of battle flags, and needle-books, and smoking-bags, women of whom the world was not worthy! These equipped us for the field and cared for us in the camp, cheered us to the battle and nursed us in the hospital. Why! the war furnished more trained nurses the first year than the schools of Christendom had in all her centuries! It raised up a host of boy scouts, women spies, and sent out scores of female blockade runners. It vacated the bench, and bar, and pulpit, and college hall, and editorial chair, and banker's desk, and mechanic's stool, and every place of sweet repose or of peaceful toil. It left the forge cold, the foundry silent, the flock untended, the field unturned, the sick to suffer alone, and weeping women to bury their devoted dead. Oh! its transforming power was marvelous. It made the old young, the weak strong, the sick well, the foreigner as the native, the sojourner as the citizen, or it made them get out of Dixie Land! Believe me, the men all went to boots and beard; the women all became angels clad in homespun; the girls cried to become boys and join the cavalry, and the boys had to be locked up to keep them from running off to Manassas. The very negroes shared the general feeling and hundreds went with young Marse to help whip "Dem Yanks." Mothers and daughters, wives and widows, sisters and sweethearts organized regular reliefs to feed, clothe, bathe, nurse, watch by, read to, write for, sing with, and pray over the wounded and bury the dead.

The war reformed society, created new classes, set new fashions, established new industries, organized new charities, gave us new ideals of duty, new tests of friendship, new charms to womanhood, new proofs of patriotism, new motives for living, new delights in dying. It fused and moulded into one solid and glorious mass the whole population, with all its sorts, sexes, sizes, orders, ranks, creeds, colors and conditions of folk, native and foreign, Protestant and Catholic, Jew and Gentile, and so made the awful engine that we called "THE ARMY," to smite and hurl back the hated, dreaded Yankee! It could be done, it had to be done; the only question was, who could help most to do it? Oh, the Southern heart was hot, it burned and blazed, and this enthusiasm, inspired its songs, winged its prayers, crowded its camps, built its ships, supported its Congress, framed its laws, created its literature and revived its religion; gave us a life worth living, a death worth dying, and a Heaven worth going to – the place of peace and rest to which no hated enemy could ever come, forever and forever! Is it strange that everybody was for it? The wonder is that anybody could stay at home. Believe me, "It robbed the cradle and the grave," so eager were our people to share its triumph or die with its defeat.

The South was never so whole-hearted, so uplifted, so self-consecrated in any cause, before or since. Never! The war feeling was not limited to the army or monopolized by the men, it was even more intense among the women. But here I must allow one of them to speak for all her own sex. I find the simple, eloquent utterance in the *Confederate Veteran* of a recent month. It is from an address of welcome made by Mrs. Sarah D. Eggleston, of Mississippi, to the United Daughters of the Confederacy, in their last annual assembly, and its simplicity and pathos are fully equalled by its truthfulness. I like it better than anything I have ever seen from the hand of man, for it manifests better the very heart of our people. The letter and spirit are all her own, and the world has none like her – The *Southern Woman!* Mrs. Eggleston says: –

The men gave, or offered to give their lives. The women gave what was dearer to them than life: they gave the men they loved. I will give some instances to prove the spirit of those women. I had a friend, a widow, who had only two sons. They both enlisted for the war. The first one was killed in the battle of Fredericksburg; the other was killed by the same volley that laid low our immortal Jackson at Chancellorsville, and this heroic boy, with his lifeblood ebbing fast, had only breath to gasp: "Is the General hurt?" When I was weeping with that poor mother, she said: "Both of my boys are gone; but if I had to do all this over again, I would not act differently.

I knew a boy who belonged to the company that was organized in the village where I am now living. When he had been in Virginia over two years and had been in many battles, his mother wrote to President Davis, using these words: "I notice that General Lee has gone into winter quarters and there will be no more fighting for several weeks; so, if my boy has done his duty, I respectfully beg that he be granted a furlough, that he may come home to me, for I greatly long to see him." Mark the simplicity and sublimity of that mother's words: "*If my boy has done his duty.*"

Bishop Polk gives an instance of the sublime devotion of a Tennessee mother who gave five sons to the Confederacy. When the first one was killed, and the Bishop was trying to say some words of comfort, she said: "My son Billy will be old enough next spring to take his brother's place." The only idea of duty that this heroic mother had was to give her sons to the cause she loved, as soon as they were old enough to bear a musket.

Such was the spirit of your mothers and your grand-
mothers.

I will tell you of two funerals that I witnessed –
one in 1861, the other in 1865. I was in New Orleans in
the early part of the summer of 1861 when I witnessed
the funeral of the gallant Colonel Charley Dreux, who
had been killed in a skirmish in Virginia before any of
the great battles had been fought. He was the first Loui-
sianian who had the honor of sealing his devotion to the
cause with his blood, and among the very first from any
State. When he was borne to his last resting place, a
vast concourse of people followed with drooping flags,
muffled drums, bands playing the dead march, and the
tolling of all the church bells of the city. It was indeed
such a funeral as befitted a hero who had died in the
defense of his country.

Far different was it, nearly four years later,
when I was in Mobile during those last sad weeks of the
war. The enemy were vigorously pushing the siege
against Spanish Fort, across the bay from Mobile. The
roar of the cannon was heard above all the noises of the
city. I was attending service in Trinity Church, for while
the men were fighting, the women were praying. The
services were progressing, and we heard the muffled
tread of feet, when, looking up, I saw eight soldiers in
their worn and faded gray, and on their shoulders was a
rude, pine coffin which contained the remains of a comrade who had been killed that morning at Spanish Fort.
The burial squad, taking their comrade for burial, had
seen the church door open, and, hearing the voice of the
minister, had gone in, that some prayers might be said
over the fallen soldier. Slowly and sadly they bore him
down the aisle, placing him at the foot of the chancel,
they standing reverently about the coffin. Without one
word, the aged minister began the burial service, all of
us joining in. We did not know over whom those prayers

were said; but we did know that he was the father, or
husband, or son, or brother, or lover of some Southern
woman, and we knew that he had died in defense of his
country. The services over and the burial squad having
removed their dead comrade from the church, the con-
gregation slowly dispersed, some of us being loath to
return to our lonely apartments. It so chanced that I was
the last person to leave the church; and when I reached
the steps, I saw a woman standing there. Doubtless she
saw in my face the same tense anxiety which I had noticed in hers, for, pointing in the direction of the Spanish
Fort, she said in a voice that I have never forgotten: "O,
listen to those guns! All that I have in this world, my
only boy is there." And I said: – "And my husband is
there too."

During the four years of the war it was my lot
to hear the guns of three besieged cities – Vicksburg,
Richmond and Mobile. I saw many partings on the eve
of battle. But seldom did I see women weep when those
farewells were taken. We parted from our loved ones
with a smile upon our lips; but when the night came, our
pillows would be wet with tears.

I have told you some things that I saw. I will
now tell you what I did not see. I saw no mother trying
to keep her boys from going into battle, I saw no wife
trying to persuade her husband not to go to the front,
and I saw no woman who cried, "*Surrender!*" If you ask
me to explain this, my answer is: – "Because we knew
we were right, our cause was just."

Comrades, does that sound like the utterance of
a politician, "a fire-eater;" or is it the voice of a Southern
woman – the revelation of her Confederate soul? Ah!
Gentlemen, it was that self-same spirit, which in the
soldier, swept the field at Shiloh, and stubbornly held the

ground at the second battle of Manassas and in "the bloody Angle," and again on the gory field of Sharpsburg, that broke the Yankee lines at Chancellorsville and sent the blue-coats flying from Chickamauga, that stormed the cannon-crowned heights of Gettysburg, and piercing the Union centre, waved the red flag of the Confederacy in the very faces of its foes! Yes, comrades, it was the *Southern woman* that was in us! God bless them forever!

CHAPTER THREE
Upon Our Part, It Was a Justifiable War
☆   ☆   ☆   ☆

The greatest calamity that can befall a State is for its people to forget its origin. – William E. Gladstone

We cannot escape History. – Abraham Lincoln

The Confederate cause was as good as the support it had; it couldn't be so now, of course, for the case is altered, the law is different; the amendments are ratified and respected; but then the Constitution had not a line in it against secession, and all analogy favored it. Secession had been frequently threatened, and once, had been actually practiced. Rhode Island is doubly distinguished, though she is the smallest of the States, she was once the champion of "State's rights." She was the last to enter "The Union," but she had been the first to secede from "The Confederation." She had entered that "Perpetual Union," in 1781, but in less than five years, in 1786, she kicked out of it, and recalled her delegates from its Congress; nor did she re-enter the family of States for four long years, or until 1790; not until she had waited two years and seven months after the adoption of the Constitution, and over a year and one-fourth after it had been ratified by the other twelve States, and was in full operation; yet no attempt was ever made to coerce her. Rhode Island's ratification was on May 29th, 1790, and even at that late day, such was her fear of imperilling her precious sovereignty that she expressly reserved the right to withdraw again, if her welfare should require it; declaring "that the powers of government may be reassumed by the people whensoever it shall become necessary to their happiness." Could South Carolina have claimed any more? Certainly, she never enacted any more, although she had more abundant provocation.

When the Louisiana Purchase was proposed in 1803, there was in the Northeast a strong dissatisfaction, because – "The influence of our part of the Union (New England) must be diminished by the acquisition of more weight at the other end." Mr. Tracy, of Connecticut, gave terse and timely expression to the Northern view and their opposition to this territorial addition, when he declared that it would result in "absorbing the Northern States and render them insignificant in the Union." Moved by that consideration, the Legislature of Massachusetts in 1804, resolved – "That the annexation of Louisiana to the Union transcends the power of United States' Government. It forms a new Confederacy, to which the States united by the former compact are not bound to adhere."

Ten years before this, Dr. Fisher Ames of Boston, a member of the Massachusetts Convention, which in 1788 had adopted our Federal Constitution, the orator, statesman, and friend of Washington, confessed that, "The spirit of insurrection has tainted a vast extent of country besides Pennsylvania." And Governor Oliver Wolcott of Connecticut, in 1796, dreading the election of

Jefferson, boldly advocated disunion. He said – "I sincerely declare that I wish the Northern States would separate from the Southern the moment the election of Jefferson shall take place." How is that for a son of Yale – a, judge of law, a Major-General in the Army, and a signer of the Declaration of Independence?

In 1805, Governor Plumer of New Hampshire acknowledged that the New England patriots entertained the purpose of breaking up the Union. The scheme was to be made good by putting a suitable man at the head of a military force strong enough to accomplish it. This conspiracy of 1803-4 was announced to all men by no less a person than John Quincy Adams over his own name – so says Dr. J. L. M. Curry and several others. A denial of it has never been heard.

Colonel T. Pickering, who was a member in good standing of Washington's Cabinet and his Postmaster General, and Secretary of State, and also a Senator from Massachusetts, was troubled somewhat over the political situation, but saw a hopeful solution. He writes – December 24, 1803, – "I will not yet despair. I will rather anticipate a new Confederacy, exempt from the corrupt and corrupting influence and oppression of the South. There will be (and our children, at farthest, will see it) a separation. The white and black population will mark the boundary." This prospect was in nowise discouraging, for the prognosticator could see neither fire nor blood. He says, "The principles of our Revolution point to the remedy – a *separation*. That this can be accomplished, and without spilling one drop of blood, I have little doubt." Such views sound strangely enough now, and down South, but one hundred and four years ago, and in the loyal (?) State of Massachusetts, they struck, with responsive moral effect, the great New England heart!

The admission of Louisiana came under discussion in 1811, when one Senator said: "If this bill passes, it is my deliberate opinion that it is a virtual dissolution of the Union; that it will free the States from their moral obligation, and as it will be the right of all, so it will be the duty of some, definitely to prepare for a separation, amicably if they can, violently, if they must." This sounds like South Carolina, but it was the speech of Honorable Josiah Quincy of Boston, and the first distinct advocacy of disunion, just fifty years before the South enacted it. An objection was raised, but no dispute made of the right. A Southern member, Mr. Poindexter objected, that, "The suggestion of a dissolution of the Union is out of order." The point was decided by the Chair *against* Mr. Quincy, but when an appeal was taken to the House, Quincy was endorsed by a two-thirds vote; so it was *not* out of order in the Congress of the United States in 1811, to avow the doctrine of even "violent" secession, provided only that it be done by sons of Massachusetts. In support of his position, Mr. Quincy said –

> Is there a principle of public law better settled, or more conformable to the plainest suggestions of reason, than that the violation of the contract by one of the parties may be considered as exempting the other from its obligations? Suppose in private life, thirteen form a partnership and ten of them undertake to admit a new partner without the concurrence of the other three. Would it not be at their option to abandon the partnership after so palpable an infringement of their rights?

When the Federal Secretary of War issued in 1812, a call for troops from Massachusetts, Rhode Island

and Connecticut, to fight against Great Britain, their governors sent him a stern refusal, and the Legislature of Connecticut in supporting the Governor, "Denounced the war, and declared that Commonwealth to be a free, and sovereign and independent State, and that the United States was not a national, but a Confederated Republic." And this novel doctrine was solemnly sanctioned by the Supreme Court of the dear old Nutmeg State! Here we see the same doctrine held and avowed and judicially sanctioned in 1812 by Connecticut that was taught by Calhoun and acted upon by South Carolina in 1860 – fifty years later!

Although made to resist the so-called "right of search," and to punish the unlawful seizure of American ships and seamen by British Captains, "the War of 1812 was generally and bitterly opposed by all New England;" at least after she felt its effects upon her commerce. The Canadian campaign was denounced "as cruel, wanton, senseless and wicked" – as "so fertile in calamities, and so threatening in its consequences, as being waged with the worst possible views, and carried on in the worst possible manner, forming a Union of wickedness and weakness, which defies for a parallel the annals of the world." Such sentiments would now consign to infamy any Southern Legislative body, but this record is opened here only because of some other sayings and doings necessary to be noticed.

The "Hartford Convention" met, December 15th, 1814, whilst Washington City was in British hands, and our Executive Mansion and Capitol lay in heaps of ashes. For three weeks it brooded over disunion measures. It failed to hatch out an ordinance of secession, but the fault was not the Convention's. The failure was due to Jackson's victory over the English at New Orleans. These original secessionists did however pass resolutions asserting a State's right of interposition, and, as President Roosevelt says, "So framed its action as to justify seceding or not seceding, as events turned out." On this point, the Convention itself said – "If secession should become necessary by reason of the multiplied abuses of bad administration, it should if possible, be the work of peaceable times, and deliberate consent." Another deliverance of this remarkable body is noteworthy. The record reads – "It is as much the duty of the State authorities to watch over the *rights reserved* as it is of the *United States to exercise the powers delegated.*" And then, to cap the climax, we have this – "In case of deliberate, dangerous, and palpable infractions of the Constitution, affecting the sovereignty of the State and liberties of the people, it is not only the right, but the duty of each State to interpose its authority for their protection." We are favored with still another wholesome utterance by the same high authority, namely, – "When emergencies occur which are beyond the reach of judicial tribunals, or too pressing to admit of the delay incident to their forms, States which have no common umpire must be their own judges, and execute their own decisions."

Among many interesting items, this orthodox assembly handed down to coming generations this deliberate decision – "that Custom duties collected in New England should be paid to the States within whose borders they were collected, and not to the United States." Mr. John Fiske, M.A., LL.D., historian, graduate of Harvard and native of Hartford, Connecticut, says, "that this would have virtually dissolved the Union."

The temper and intention of these able and honored leaders of public opinion may be learned from the published testimony of Governor Plumer of New Hampshire. He writes, –

> I am certain that, upon retiring early one evening from dining with Aaron Burr, Mr. Hilhouse said in an animated tone, "The Eastern States must and will dissolve the Union, and form a separate Government of their own: and the sooner they do this the better." I think that the first man who mentioned the subject of a dismemberment was Samuel Hunt, a representative of New Hampshire. But there was no man with whom I conversed so often, so freely and fully as with Robert Griswold. He was, without doubt, or hesitation, decidedly in favor of dissolving the Union, and establishing a Northern Confederacy.

This "treasonable convention" – as John Quincy Adams calls it – representing, by the amplest Legislative authority, the Five New England States (Maine was not a State then), did not believe the times quite ripe for their movement, and so adjourned to meet in Boston, on June, 1815, to hear the report of its commissioners who had been sent with complaints to Washington. The expected report didn't come. The re-assembling never happened. Peace put an end to the project. Otherwise the first secession ordinance would have been put to the credit of Massachusetts, and not of South Carolina!

This same spirit prevailed and showed itself in the North, again and again without rebuke. On January 24, 1842, John Quincy Adams and Joshua R. Giddings presented petitions from citizens of Massachusetts and Ohio, asking Congress to take steps toward the peaceable dissolution of the Union. These petitions were stoutly opposed by Mr. Gilmore of Virginia, and Mr. Marshall of Kentucky, who brought in resolutions censuring Mr. Adams for presenting them; but after two long weeks of sharp discussion, the House by a big majority laid on the table the resolutions, thus showing that the movers had done no wrong and the petitioners asked nothing treasonable or unlawful. Mr. Adams was a bold defender of the right of secession. In a speech made in 1839, before the New York Historical Society, among other such statements is this – "Under these limitations have the people of each State in the Union a right to secede from the Confederated Union itself." Did Messrs. Davis, Toombs, Rhett or Yancey ever say more?

The admission of Texas was claimed to fully justify disunion. The acquisition of Florida also, while less resisted, "resulted in our getting less territory from Spain than she was ready to yield, just to avoid irritating New England." The chronic trouble was a territorial one – to put it in the words of George Bancroft, a Massachusetts man, a graduate of Harvard, the most laborious and elaborate historian of our country, a man who spent fifty years upon his ponderous volumes – the trouble was – "An ineradicable dread of the coming power of the Southwest lurked in New England, especially in Massachusetts." Only the treaty of peace with old England, signed at Ghent by Henry Clay in 1814, prevented the formation of a New England Confederacy with its Capital at Boston. Believe me, there were men once who deplored the peace made at Ghent!

Again in 1844, Charles F. Adams introduced in the Massachusetts Legislature a resolution almost the same as that of Mr. Quincy in 1811, and said – "Massachusetts is determined to submit to undelegated powers

in no body of men on earth, and the project of the annexation of Texas, unless arrested upon the threshold, may
tend to drive these States into a dissolution of the Union."
Adopted. Of such utterances the half has ne'er been told!

Four years before the Charleston Convention met
to dissolve the bond that connected South Carolina with
the other States, a secession convention sat in Worcester,
Massachusetts, and on January 15, 1857, *"Resolved,* That
the sooner the separation takes place, the more peaceable
it will be; but that peace or war is a secondary consideration. Slavery must be conquered; peaceably if we can,
forcibly if we must." Henry Ward Beecher is recorded as
saying – "It will be an advantage for the South to go off."
In celebrating the glorious Fourth, July, 1854, William
Lloyd Garrison "publicly burned a copy of the United
States Constitution with the words – THE UNION MUST
BE DISSOLVED."

Horace Greeley's great paper, the *New York Tribune,* in an editorial of November 9th, 1860, said –

> If the Cotton States shall decide that they can do
> better out of the Union than in it, we insist on letting
> them go in peace. The right to secede may be a revolu-
> tionary one, but it exists nevertheless. Whenever a con-
> siderable section of our Union shall deliberately resolve
> to go out, we shall resist all coercive measures designed
> to keep it in. We hope never to live in a Republic where
> one section is pinned to the residue by bayonets.

The next year in New Bedford, Massachusetts, the
most rabid of politicians, – Wendell Phillips – declared –
"The States that think their peculiar institutions require a
separate government have a right to decide that question
without appealing to you or me." Alas! for his logic. For

long years after this, he supported every bloody attempt of government to deny to eleven sovereign States the very right that he himself had allowed. The number and variety of such sayings is about endless, and as I am not making a book, but only a speech, I desist.

The right to secede, so freely asserted, and so strongly held by the North, was not prohibited by any word of the Constitution. In the Articles of Confederation it had been plainly denied. The last sentence in that document is this – *"That this Union be perpetual!"* But the Constitution has no such declaration. The duration of the Union was left by its authors to the future free choice of the States that had voluntarily entered it. The limitations of the Constitution bear chiefly upon the powers of the Federal Government. Consider the Tenth Amendment – "The powers not delegated to the United States by the Constitution, nor prohibited by it to the States, are *reserved to the States, respectively,* or to the people." Now, since the power to secede isn't denied by the Constitution to the States; and since the power to coerce a State is nowhere delegated to the Federal Government; it follows that its exercise was optional and perfectly lawful. The Declaration of Independence had been made and signed by the colonies acting separately and as sovereign powers, "not by the people as a whole, nor by a majority of the whole people." Their independence had been acknowledged by Great Britain, not as the independence of a new "nation," but as the freedom of separate and sovereign States, each receiving recognition by her colonial name; and the Constitution had been framed, not by "a mixed multitude," or a sectional majority, or by a popular vote of citizens of all the States, but by a vote of *the States,* as such, each State casting one vote; and this action of each State was later ratified in her own convention of her own delegates, and of her own free will. The freedom of the South came not by the grace of Yankee Doodle, but by the proclamation of King George, the Third, and he granted it to Virginia – not to an "entire nation," but severally, to each State – to Virginia, the Carolinas, Georgia and the others.

Knowing that these States, thus "united," were free and sovereign when they were still separate colonies, when they won their independence, when they adopted severally and separately the Constitution, our statesmen supposed that they were still as legally and morally free to go out, as they had been to come in; and that it lay in their own breasts to abide in, or depart from, the Union. That they had enslaved themselves when they ratified the Constitution, was not dreamed of; that they had made unconsciously a great governmental machine of higher power than they themselves possessed, would have been scouted as nonsense, since the creature cannot be greater than its creator! If the power to do doesn't imply the power to undo, they believed it did. That the Federal Government, the servant of all, of only delegated powers, for specific purposes, had become the sole sovereign, with inherent rights, superior to those of the States that gave it being, would have seemed to them absurd and impossible! The Declaration of Independence was not made by a Nation, or by a Union, but by thirteen separate and sovereign colonies. Foreign powers – France, in 1778, Sweden in 1783, and the Netherlands, in 1782 – had entered into treaties with them, not as one "national government," but with each as a sovereign State. And Great Britain did not acknowledge their independence as a "united people," but as politically distinct and sovereign

States, designating each by her chosen name. Roger Sherman, of Connecticut, said in the Convention of 1787: "Foreign States have made treaties with us as confederated *States,* and *not* as a National Government." Now, if these States, so united, had that character when they declared their independence, when they won their freedom, when they severally ratified their Constitution, *pray when, and how did they lose it?* They not only had this sovereignty, but were zealous to keep it, when in their Conventions they agreed to unite as States, they "reserved" to themselves all rights and powers not delegated to the Federal Government; and some asserted in plain terms the right to resume them, whenever their welfare called for it. This was the saving clause of the ratification of the Constitution by Virginia, Pennsylvania, New York, Rhode Island, New Hampshire, North and South Carolina and Massachusetts.

The last named, in her State constitution, has embalmed for coming ages a declaration of her immutable faith in her own inviolable and supreme sovereignty worthy of world-wide fame. It runs as follows – "The people of this Commonwealth have the sole and exclusive right of governing themselves as a free, sovereign and independent State; and do, and shall forever hereafter exercise and enjoy every power and jurisdiction and right which is not, nor may not hereafter be, by them, expressly delegated to the United States." "O! Jew, I thank thee for that word!" No clearer, sounder political doctrine was ever sent forth by man: and this was ordained and published in Massachusetts, A.D. 1792, five years *after* her ratification of our Federal compact. In the Union she is still asserting sovereign and independent statehood!

The thought of an actual secession from the Union

by an aggrieved State may not have had any large place in the minds of those who made our Constitution, but the idea of failure in duty, and of nullification of law did occur to some persons and a proposal to give Congress the power "to call forth the force of the Union against any member of it failing to fulfill its duty" was actually made and *voted down,* Mr. Madison moved to postpone the question. This was agreed to by a unanimous vote, and the matter never came up again. George Mason, (whom Thomas Jefferson said, was the wisest man that he ever knew), speaking of the use of force, asked; – "Will not the citizens of the invaded State assist one another, until they rise up as one man and shake off the Union altogether?" In the Convention of New York, Alexander Hamilton declared: –

> To coerce the State is one of the maddest projects that was ever devised. What picture does this idea present to our view? A complying State at war with a non-complying State: Congress marching the troops of one State into the bosom of another! Here is a nation at war with itself! Can any reasonable man be well disposed toward a government which makes war and carnage the only means of supporting itself? A government that can exist only by the sword? But can we believe that one State will ever suffer itself to be used as an instrument of coercion? The thing is a dream! It is impossible!

Alas! In 1861, this dreadful dream became an awful reality.

Long before May 14, 1787, the date of the Convention that framed our Federal Constitution, and in that Convention, as well, and ever since it, there were, and there are still, two governmental ideas and two opposing political parties supporting them. At different times, these have had different names, leaders, motives, methods and ends to be gained, which of course led to the adoption of different policies according to the different purposes to be served. Alexander Hamilton was the gifted leader of one of these parties, and Thomas Jefferson was the sagacious statesman representing the other. The first party favored the establishment of a strong, centralized, national, Federal Government. The second as sincerely contended for the sovereignty of the States, which were soon to become politically united. With the first, the Union was to have superior strength and real supremacy. With the second, the States were to retain and exercise their free, independent and sovereign rights, the power of local self-government. They were to remain, as before, each one politically unhampered in the control of her own domestic concerns, as free within the league, as she had been without it, except as to certain powers specified and delegated in the compact to the Federal Government for the common welfare. From the earliest times there had existed among the States a widespread distrust of government and fear of oppression from it, engendered, it may be, by colonial experience of British tyranny. In the smaller States, this grew later into a deep dread of interference by the more powerful States, and great carefulness to guard against it is abundantly manifest. The constitutional provision of equal power in the Senate for every State is evidently due to this natural feeling. This fear increased as legislation and experience in the Union developed diverse interests and sectional antipathies. Conflict was natural and seemed unavoidable. Geographical position, soil, climate, pursuits, domestic habits and environment, religious notions and political institutions, social antecedents and racial affinities, commercial interests and foreign immigration – all these combined to bring forth and foster the mutual dread, aversion and jealousy which ended in our sectional struggle – our fratricidal war. The North was most dependent upon trade and commerce, fisheries, mills, mines and manufactories. The South was most interested in cattle, sheep, hogs, horses, grain, rice, sugar, cotton, indigo, tobacco and other farm products. It was rural in taste, habit, interest, everything. The North was urban, given to trading and making things, to moving and money getting. Our people loved nature and cultivated the soil, raised horses, followed the dogs, handled the guns, founded families, and lived like lords, whether in cabins or manor-houses, and called these abodes – "home-sweet home." In the North, a mixed multitude united in trades-union, guilds and lodges; in the South, a native, homogeneous people, widely separated, and personally, independent, lived largely alone, and each as he liked. One had negro slaves and cared kindly for them: the other sold him those slaves, and despised and denounced slavery! – having found it quite unprofitable!

These local and constitutional differences produced diverse domestic, social and industrial demands: and these led to legislation intended to protect and promote the welfare of each section. And so, a political struggle was engendered. The questions of territorial expansion, protective tariffs, and African servitude brought on at length the "irrepressible conflict." Upon both sides it was a struggle for power – "The balance of power" – to be wielded for local, material interests, to preserve domestic peace and secure sectional glory. The North fought for supremacy. The South contended for the Constitution which was her only hope of salvation.

Both sections claimed support in the Constitution. The North contended that the Federal Government was made by "the people of the United States;" that the adoption of our Constitution merged the States into a "NATION," and gave to its Congress supreme power. Daniel Webster said: "The Constitution itself, in its very front, declares, that it was ordained and established by the people of the United States in the aggregate." He refers to the "Preamble," *but it declares no such thing!* He put in just what "the Fathers" had carefully left out of it, viz. *"in the aggregate."* True, it says. "We, the people of the United States, in order to form a more perfect union, etc." But this "people" is the people composing the several States, and not the whole mass of citizens living in all the geographical extent of the Union. The South holds that the Constitution is a *compact* made by free and sovereign *States,* each one of whom approved it by her own individual vote; that this contract was ratified later by the people of each State, in her Convention assembled, and that in so doing no State surrendered her rights or power of self-government, except as to such powers as were specified in the document, and which were granted by the framers of it to the Federal Agent, for the defense, welfare and happiness of all the States.

There arose, of course, the question of origin and intention of the Constitution itself. How, and by whom, was it made, and what is its meaning? History alone can answer, and it does answer, and its answer is an ample, clear, complete vindication of the political action of our people, and of their struggle to maintain it on a thousand bloody fields.

When the great Convention at Philadelphia had

ended its immortal work, the original document was en-
trusted to a "Committee on Style," that the *i's* should be
dotted, and the *t's* crossed; that the grammar and rhetoric
should be perfected, in order that the mind of the makers
should be exactly expressed. Now, in reviewing the "PRE-
AMBLE," a verbal difficulty came to mind. As it was first
drawn, the Preamble contained the name of every State
that had engaged in its construction; but according to its
express terms, the Constitution needed the consent of
only *nine* States for its adoption, and to give it legal operative force: and hence the Committee naturally and rightly
judged that the Preamble should contain only the names
of those States which would sanction and accept the paper. It seemed to the Committee grossly improper to in-
sert in the compact the names of parties that might not
afterwards agree to it. But *which* of the Thirteen would
agree to it? No human being could foresee. So, rather
than risk a guess, and probably miss some State which
would ratify the work, and rather than leave an ugly and
unexplained blank in the head-piece of the instrument, the
Committee decided to substitute for the several names of
States the phrase – *"We, the people of the United States,
&c.,"* leaving to time and to the action of the States, to
add the proper signatures belonging thereto. If the Fathers of the Republic had been prophets as well as patriots, they would have surely said – *"We, the States of
America,* do ordain, &c, &c." Alas! they were not
inspired. Having done its work, the Committee laid it
before the House, on September the twelfth, 1787, and it
was adopted without dissent. The rough original of the
Preamble, containing the name of every State, had been
already unanimously approved, on August the sixth, and
for over a month had remained unaltered; now, is it at all

probable that the little verbal change made in one phrase could have been accepted by the Convention without dispute or division, if it was to work the Monstrous Machine imagined by Mr. Webster? Had such an effect been even suspected at the time it would have created consternation, and the record of it would remain. I can find in the account no resistance whatever. Nor can I believe that, at the last moment, the wicked attempt was made to destroy the liberty of the States by fusing into one political mass thirteen separate Sovereignties which for four months had fought for their inherent political rights. If such action could have transformed these States into a "NATION," and if that was done, pray how came the trick to be turned without a word of protest from the mighty men who from the first had feared such a fate? How could so many earnest, eloquent men sit in solemn silence and witness and consent to the death of State Sovereignty? Of course, they never did it. No such attempt was ever allowed or thought of.

The reason for the use of the phrase – *"We, the people of the United States"* – was just this – Nine States could form the compact, and put into full force the Constitution; but no body could tell which nine would do so. The framers, therefore, could consistently name no State: but rather than leave a suspicious blank on the fair face of the immortal Document, they met the demand by using the words – *"We, the people of the United States,"* the sense being, – we, the people of such States as shall hereafter ratify and ordain it. Nothing else could have been done. How could the Convention have left in the Preamble the name of Rhode Island, for example, when she had no representative in the Convention Hall, and when its wonderful work did not find acceptance with that cautious little Commonwealth for several anxious years, and only then by the very slim majority of two votes out of sixty-six that were cast? Even New York, urged on by the powerful influence of Alexander Hamilton, assented by a majority of only three votes – thirty to twenty-seven. The phrase is explained and justified by every circumstance in the case, except to such men as are wilfully blind. But Oh! what *things* are *words.* "Out of one foolish word may start a thousand daggers," says Jeremy Bentham. Ah! these few fateful words – what "woes unnumbered" sprang from them!

> But words are things and a small drop of ink,
> Falling, like dew, upon a thought, produces
> That which makes thousands, perhaps millions, think.

So Byron thought and wrote! Should *we* not think? It is claimed that the adoption of the Constitution made of us a consolidated "NATION." This is clearly disproved both by the mode of its ratification and the specified condition upon which it was to become operative. It must be ratified by the peoples of the *States,* and it required *nine* such ratifications to give it validity among them. If we are, or ever were, "one people" *en masse*, then we must have been made so by a majority vote of the whole population. And that vote must have overruled any minority, no matter where cast or by whom counted. Did such election ever occur? Where, when, how, and by what means and authority was any such vote ever taken? The only action ever had in reference to the Constitution was the action of the *States,* each in her own time, and place, and manner, and in words of her own choosing, and by delegates of her own selection. If that wasn't the *modus operandi* of our making as these "United States," let those who know some other declare it. If the majority of the entire population might, and did, establish our Federal Government over the whole land, why was the assent of only "nine States" made necessary to its ordination and operation? And why did George Mason, William Grayson and Patrick Henry resist so stoutly in the Virginia Convention its ratification even after the necessary "nine" had approved it? According to the theory of Webster, Story, Motley, Bancroft, Everett and Curtis, the Constitution was even then the law in Virginia, and it was treasonable conduct to oppose it, for it had been already ratified by Delaware, Pennsylvania, New Jersey, Georgia, Connecticut, Massachusetts, Maryland, South Carolina and New Hampshire, while the Virginians were yet weighing it in the balance of liberty. Who are to be trusted as expounders of the Constitution, the men who made it, or those who called themselves to the task of interpretation sixty years afterwards? Mr. Madison made this reply to Patrick Henry when he stood in opposition to Virginia's adoption of it because of this very Preamble:

> Who are parties to the Constitution? "The people" – but not the people as composing one great body, but the people as composing *thirteen sovereignties:* were it a consolidated government, the assent of a majority of the people would be sufficient for its establishment, and as a majority have adopted it already, the remaining States would be bound by the acts of the majority, even if they unanimously reprobated it: were it such a government, it would be now binding upon the people of this State, without their having had the privilege of deliberating upon it; but sir, no State is bound by it, as it is, without its own consent.

And "Light-Horse Harry" Lee, in the same strain

replied, – "The Constitution is now submitted *to the people of Virginia.* If we do not adopt it, it will always be null and void as to us." This is quite conclusive. This at once silenced Henry and Mason and Grayson. It doesn't leave a grain of sand for Webster or Motley or Story or Everett or Bancroft or Curtis to stand on.

Is our Government national, or is it a co-partnership of equal and sovereign States? *"That is the question."* Having heard Webster, may we not now listen to Washington? General Washington, our own glorious Washington, the President of the Philadelphia Convention and the First Chief Magistrate of our Union should surely have known the nature of the government that he was to administer and that he had helped to make. In writing to Count Rochambeau, on January 8, 1788, he says: "The Constitution is to be submitted to conventions chosen by the people in the several States and by them approved or rejected." Who knew, Washington or Webster? General Lafayette also had from Washington on April 28, 1788, this line – *"The people of the several States* (not of the entire country, nor "in the aggregate") retain everything they do not by express terms, give up." Did they ever in express terms, or otherwise, give up their sovereignty, or their right to rule and regulate their own internal affairs? NEVER!

A fact very significant of the nature of our government is recorded by Dr. J. L. M. Curry, to wit: –

At one time in the progress of framing the Constitution, the words – "National Government" were used twenty-six times in a committee report. Next day Mr. Ellsworth of Connecticut moved to strike out the words, "National Government" and to use the words – "Government of United States." This was unanimously agreed to, and the term "National" forever disappeared from our great Charter; leaving us, beyond all doubt, a Government that is Federal and not National.

The theory of the centralizationists was stubbornly advocated by Webster, and later by Story, Everett, Bancroft, Motley and others, but Mr. Henry Cabot Lodge, a Boston politician and orator, a Harvard graduate, a Senator from Massachusetts, biographer of Alexander Hamilton, Daniel Webster, editor of the *North American Review* and historian-at-large, confesses that –

It was probably necessary, at all events Mr. Webster felt it to be so, to argue that the Constitution, at the outset, was not a contract between the States, but a National instrument. Unfortunately the *facts were against him.* When the Constitution was adopted by the votes of the States at Philadelphia, and accepted by the votes of States in popular conventions, it is safe to say that there was not a man in the country from Washington and Hamilton on the one side, to George Clinton and George Mason on the other, who regarded the new system as anything but an experiment entered upon by the *States,* and *from which each and every State had the right peaceably to withdraw,* a right which was very likely to be exercised.

Certainly this conclusion is one from which Mr. Lodge can never be dislodged; for facts are more than "stubborn" – they are eternal!

Mr. Webster and Justice Joseph Story both of the same loyal State virtually admit that if our Constitution be a compact between the States, the States would have the right to withdraw from it at pleasure; "even" says Webster (in his debate with Calhoun in 1833), "Although it might be one of its stipulations that it should be perpetual." To prove the right of secession then according to this great interpreter of the Constitution, it is only necessary to establish the fact that the Constitution is a *"Compact."* A single sentence from the act of ratification by Massachusetts of the Federal Constitution is quite conclusive. She "acknowledges with grateful hearts the goodness of the Supreme Ruler of the Universe, in affording the people of the United States the opportunity deliberately and peaceably, without fraud or surprise, of entering into an explicit and solemn *compact* with each other, &c." This testimony of the Massachusetts Senator, Lodge, and of the Bay State itself, sitting in deliberate and peaceful counsel is heavy evidence against Webster, "the great expounder;" but it is positively shocking to see him refute himself! In 1819, December 15, he presented in the United States Congress a Memorial from citizens of Boston, endorsed by himself as chairman of the Committee, in which he speaks of the States as enjoying *"the exclusive possession of sovereignty* over their own territory." He calls the United States – "the American Confederacy." He says, "The only parties to the Constitution, contemplated by it originally, were *the Thirteen Confederated States."*

In his famous speech at Capon Springy, Virginia, delivered over thirty years later, Webster declared: "I have not hesitated to say, and I repeat, that, if the Northern States refuse wilfully and deliberately, to carry into effect that part of the Constitution which respects the restoration of fugitive slaves, and Congress provide no remedy, the *South would be no longer bound to observe the Compact.* A bargain cannot be broken on one side and still bind the other side." Had Webster lived but ten years longer, he must have become a secessionist, or shown himself very inconsistent indeed. If he could rise from the dead, and confront his Capon Springs speech, he would scarcely deny, at any rate, "*the compact*" contained in it. "But neither will they be persuaded though one rose from the dead."

That Alexander Hamilton was a pretty good believer in strong government was never questioned. Yet he clearly recognized the States as sovereign parties to the contract. In the *Federalist*, he writes – "Every Constitution for the United States must inevitably consist of a great variety of particulars, in which thirteen independent States are to be accommodated in their interests or opinions of interest. Hence the necessity of moulding and arranging all the particulars, which are to compose the whole, in such a manner as to satisfy *all the parties to the compact.*" Are not these parties, "The Thirteen Independent States?" Again, he calls the new Union, *"The Confederacy"* – himself using capitals for emphasis.

But why record men's names to determine a point that is plainly established by the document itself? The VIIth Article should end all controversy. "The ratification of the conventions of nine *States* shall be sufficient for the establishment of this Constitution between the *States* so ratifying the same." Not between the inhabitants of all the territory – not between the various communities or municipalities of this continent; but *"between the States* so ratifying."* The States are the parties, and it is *their* ratification that "establishes" the compact.

To show that the true doctrine is absolutely invulnerable, and positively indubitable, I add just one more fact of record – in the Philadelphia Convention, on July 23, 1787, it was Gouverneur Morris, of Pennsylvania, who "moved that the reference of the plan (of Constitution) be made to one General Convention, chosen and authorized by the people, to consider, amend and establish the same." Oh! what a time that was for a Webster! He might have won immortality by seconding the motion. Of all human history, that was the fateful hour in which to advocate and ordain a government for the mass, and by the mass. But – The Convention didn't want that. They wouldn't have it, and no man came to the rescue. Mr. Morris' proposal did not reach a vote. The record is, *"not seconded,"* and "the Father of the Constitution," Mr. Madison, makes the record. And he too speaks of the New Union as *"Confederated States."* Madison! Think of it! and Morris of Pennsylvania!

In view of these facts and declarations by the authors of the Constitution, how strange and absurd is Mr. Lincoln's theory of March 4, 1861 that, *"The Union is older than any of the States, and, in fact, it created them as States."* How could the adoption of the Constitution *create* States, when according to the document itself, nine *States,* acting as such, must first accept it to give it any legal force? Consistency here would require the "States" to enact the Constitution, which must give them being, before they themselves could have existence!!

The question was once asked Mr. Lincoln – "Why not let the South go?" He exclaimed – "Let the South go! *Where then shall we get our revenue?"* The President knew far more of the practical benefits of our tax and tariff systems than of the fundamental principles of the Federal Government.

Mr. Lincoln should certainly have credit for his clear understanding of one point, and for his perfectly positive and distinct avowal that he would not act contrary to his convictions in regard to it. In passing, I wish to accord him this honor. I refer to his statement in his first inaugural address, concerning his position upon the slave question. He said, "I have no purpose, directly or indirectly to interfere with the institution of slavery in the States where it exists. I believe I have no lawful right to do so, and I have no inclination to do so." Whether Lincoln was in this sincere, or simply shrewd, can not, of course, be known until all hearts are made manifest. The thing that we do know is – within about eighteen months, he emancipated by his own proclamation all the slaves living in the seceded States! As a "war measure" it was not unwise; as regards the Constitution, it was utterly without reason or right. He himself said, "I have no lawful right to interfere with the institution of slavery." Then how came he to be clothed with the lawful right to do it, on or before "September 22nd, 1862;" and who gave it to him? Echo answers – Who? Two billion of dollars' worth of slaves were made free without compensation or lawful right, according to the *Encyclopedia of the United States History*, by Harper Bros., 1902.

Slavery was not the cause of the war, "any more than the tax on tea was the cause of the American revolution;" but it was the occasion of secession, for it was the matter that the Abolitionists could never let alone. Some seventy years ago, they presented through John Quincy Adams in Congress, in one day, five hundred and eleven petitions for the abolition of slavery. It had existed from the beginning in every colony and was popular in Massachusetts a century before the Declaration of Independence. Those pious people had bought cargoes of slaves of the Dutch, and had sold into bondage their Pequod Indian prisoners; but bye the bye, they found it more lucrative to trade their gin and rum for black men in Africa, and to sell these black cargoes to planters in the Carolinas and Georgia, and so it was done. The Constitution expressly recognized this property, which the Dutch in 1619, and later the English and the Puritans, had sold us, and provided for the safe return of all fugitives to the State from which they had fled. (Article IV, Section 2.) New England, moreover, had a fugitive slave law in 1643; or 145 years before the Federal Constitution was adopted. But returning slaves to *her* soil is one thing; and *her* returning them to *us* is quite another thing!

Bad as Southern slavery may have been, it was our inheritance. Mr. R. E. Lee, Jr., well says – "Slavery was the South's calamity and not her crime." It descended upon us from the Pilgrim Fathers and our old English ancestors, and in spite of its evils, it was the mildest form of servitude ever found among men. I shall not apologize for the dead institution. I cannot defend its Dutch promotors, or New England dealers, but I will say that, it did for the negro far more than any other labor system had ever done for any other savage since the world was! It gave him soap and made him wash. It redeemed him from barbarism and idolatry, made him human, gave him a home and told him of Heaven. It clothed and fed him. It protected him in his ignorance, fostered him in infancy, trained him in youth, cared for him in sickness, sheltered and comforted him in old age, and at death gave him Christian burial. It restrained his passions, reformed his indolent, indecent habits, created his conscience, inspired his faith and filled him with hope. It tolerated no idleness, insolence, intemperance, disorder or lawlessness. It made no paupers, or beggars, or tramps, or rapists of women and children, turned out of home no widows, orphans, or worn-out parents. It promoted peace, quietness and good government. It trained black men and women for useful living as no industrial schools have ever done before or since, and did it without expense or de-moralization of master or servant! State laws, with regard for social standing and self-interest, all combined to pre-vent cruel treatment of these bond servants, and, indeed, rendered it quite rare; the idle, insolent and vicious alone feeling the lash. The negro who did his work even moder-ately well and behaved himself, did not lack food or fire, or friends, or home, or clothes, or medicine or the protec-tion of law. He had baker and butcher, tailor and shoe-maker, doctor and preacher, without money and without price. The master was no monster. The servant was no terror. And lighter labor seldom obtained as great com-forts. The spirit, and example, and discipline of Mistress and Master – not to mention their humanity, sympathy, kindness, refinement and Christian conduct in the planta-tion home – operated to create a bond of friendship in the family – a measure of confidence in the owner and a de-gree of trustworthiness in the slave – that was the wonder and admiration of all who had knowledge of it. During the war, it stood the test of money and power – of fire and sword – of offered freedom and promised fortune!

And it was not considered criminal to be a slave-holder even in New England in those brave old days. The Puritans both held and sold slaves. Dr. Charles Hodge, Princeton President, and great teacher of Theology, even as late as the year 1860, was constrained to confess, at the risk of his place and popularity, that –

> When Southern Christians are told that they are guilty of a heinous crime, worse than piracy, robbery, or murder, because they hold slaves, when they know that Christ and his Apostles never denounced slave-holding as a crime, never called upon men to renounce it as a condition of admission to the Church, they are shocked

and offended without being convinced. The argument from the conduct of Christ and his immediate followers seems to us decisive upon the point that slave-holding in itself considered is not a crime.

Rev. George Whitefield, the eloquent Wesleyan Evangelist, held in his orphanage and on his farm in Georgia, in 1775, seventy-five negroes, which he left by will to the Countess of Huntington. Bishop Berkley, of Rhode Island, was also a slave-owner. The famous preacher and theologian, whose great name is still good to conjure with, the mighty Jonathan Edwards, with other property, left a negro boy. (The "bill of sale" for him may still be seen.) Those pious people bought and sold slaves without the least regard to ties of blood. And one historian says – "The giving away of little negroes as soon as weaned was then a common civility, much as it now is for one to present his friend with a puppy." A Boston paper of that period has this advertisement, "A likely negro woman about nineteen years old and child about sixteen months, to be sold together or apart." Such notices were very common. The same author gives other advertisements as illustrations of the fact that the Puritans preferred to *buy* rather than to *rear* their slaves. It was a cheaper and, well – that is reason enough. This notice is from the *Continental Journal,* March 1st, 1781 – "To be sold an extraordinary likely Negro Wench, seventeen years old. She can be warranted to be strong, healthy and good natured, has no notion of Freedom, has always been used to a Farmer's Kitchen and Dairy, and is not known to have any failings, but being with child which is the only cause of her being sold." Child-slaves were sold by the pound, in New England, as pigs and other live stock are now.

A French refugee in "the cradle of liberty," writes home, "You may also here own negroes and negresses, and there is not a house in Boston, however small may be its means, that has not one or two." The State of Georgia gave to General Anthony Wayne of the Quaker State, a rice plantation in token of appreciation of his heroic services during the war with England, and this led the veteran to borrow $20,000 "with which to stock his plantation with negroes." Why not, if it was right to sell Pequot Indian prisoners as slaves, and to send them away to the Bermudas, and if the Puritans had done that, one hundred and fifty in a batch, with the orphan and widow of Philip, their mighty Chief, how could it be wrong for "Mad Anthony" to buy thirty or forty negro field-hands to raise rice in Georgia, seeing that they had all been reared as slaves, and not like the Indians born freemen? General Wayne was no better man than General Washington, and he had about 300 bond slaves, born in his house and bought with his money.

Massachusetts, always aggressive, had done much more than send away her aboriginal American freemen to be sold into slavery. She was the pioneer for all who penetrated the African jungle to capture and transport as slaves to free America the native children of the dark Continent. One of the first ships that she ever launched and employed in this business was christened, *Desire* – a name expressing well the colonial feeling for the uplift of a degraded race, and – for the revenue arising therefrom! This philanthropic adventure, this infant industry, required no protective tariff or subsidy for its encouragement. It flourished from the first, for it had the prayers of the saints and "the Colony was the principal in the business." At the start, the stolen negroes were sold in the West Indies, but later along all our Southern coast line. New York shared honors and profits with New England in thus doing good to the "brother in black," and they (so says their historian) "practically monopolized the traffic for many years." A hundred years later, when experience had shown slavery to be unprofitable in the North, and that free negroes were a "dead-weight" and nuisance among them, idle, improvident and vicious, we can see a strong antipathy developing for everything connected with slavery. Legislation now turned against it, and State by State, it was outlawed. The poor negro became himself an object of disgust, suspicion and petty persecution. There was scant room for him. In Connecticut, Miss Prudence Crandall's negro girls' school was mobbed, and so damaged that she had to give it up. The Legislature, on May 24, 1833, passed a "black law" by which all such Christian efforts were "practically prohibited." The ringing of bells and firing of cannons gave vent to the public approbation. The godly lady-teacher who had been locked up in prison was released, but her house was set on fire, and the opposition so strongly shown that she abandoned her educational efforts. Two years earlier, a negro male school in New Haven had encountered the same fate. In New Hampshire, "Noyes Academy" for negroes was closed out, because "the respectable people of the town were so incensed" that they pulled down the house. No "common schools" would admit colored children. All public conveyances were closed against them. On steamers and sailboats they had to go as steerage or deck-passengers, or not go at all. The "Jim Crow" apartment was found even in God's house, and Sambo and Dinah must take backseats. In Boston, "The cradle of Liberty," an Ethiopian pew-holder had his own pew-door nailed fast to keep him out for the awful crime of failing to "change his skin." In the great church of Dr. Storrs, no pew-deed might be made except "to respectable *white* persons." The color line was drawn as distinctly in Boston as in New Orleans! and drawn in His house with whom there is "no respect of persons!"

But with this spreading and deepening aversion for the person and presence of the negro, strange as it certainly is, there began to come a lot of legislation in favor of his freedom. Whether this was due to sympathy with Sambo, or to antipathy for his master, or both, "deponent saith not." To free the other man's slave may have seemed easier to the brother who had sold his own, and also more obligatory. In the year 1808, the American traffic in slaves from foreign shores ceased by legal limitation, and any person caught engaged in it was to be deemed guilty of piracy. In 1820, in the adoption of the Missouri compromise, the geographical extension of slavery beyond 36° 30', north latitude, was prohibited. In Virginia's Convention of 1830, but few votes were lacking to procure prospective emancipation. And many a philanthropist and Christian had arranged to free his slaves whenever the laws should allow him. Such was the tenor of the will of Mrs. Lee's father concerning his family servants, and five years after his death, in 1863, his executor. General R. E. Lee, sent all these dark-skinned dependents through his military lines as freedmen and women, at liberty to go wherever they liked. It is now certain, and never denied that slavery would in the course of events have been peaceably abolished, and with just legal compensation of owners, but for the rabid utterances and wicked antagonisms excited by the Abolition leaders throughout the North.

Dr. Hunter McGuire, the Chief Surgeon of General Jackson's Division, has published the statement that both Lee and Jackson "were in favor of freeing all the slaves in the South," and of paying for them after our independence had been achieved. He also makes this declaration – "I know that I am within proper bounds when I assert that, there was not one soldier in thirty who owned, or ever expected to own, a slave." A recent official report declares that "more than 80 per cent, of our Confederate soldiers owned no slaves." It is everywhere known that General Joe Johnston never owned a slave, although something of a Southern soldier. And it might as well be known that General U. S. Grant did own slaves until they were made free by Mr. Lincoln's proclamation. In the light of such facts, how supremely absurd does the saying of a Northern historian sound, namely, "Slavery was the cause of the war, just as property is the cause of robbery." Granting, however, that this historian is correct in assigning the motive of the robbery, it can scarcely be claimed that the South fought so long and so hard for the property held by only one in thirty of her gallant defenders. The historian is clearly an ignorant person or a worse character.

Mr. Webster said, March 7, 1850, "The South in my judgment is right and the North is wrong." In July, he declared, "The prejudice against the Southern labor system all originates in misinformation, false representations, and misapprehensions, arising from labored efforts made in the last twenty years to pervert the public judgment and irritate the public feeling." Mr. Webster was Senator for Massachusetts.

In the year 1852, a book called *Uncle Tom's Cabin* was published by Mrs. Harriett Beecher Stowe of

New England. "Designed to illustrate the horrors of African slavery," and skillfully constructed so as to appeal strongly to the reader's imagination, conscience and prejudice, this story had an enormous run. In five years, its sales amounted to a half million copies. It was "pushed" by every agency known to the trade, the church and the Abolition party. It found credulous readers among all classes and in all countries. There was in it as much money as morals, and the money as well as the morals met in the North a long-felt want. The novel later was dramatized and made a "piteous spectacle" for gaping crowds. Then, of course, actors, artists, managers, lecturers, reviewers, publishers, newspapers, bill-posters, and the like, began to hear the cry of the downtrodden children of Ham and to feel very keenly the awful crime of slave-holding. Tender translators next took up the tale of woe and soon its powerful pathos was felt throughout Germany, France, Italy, Austria, England, Ireland, Scotland – in fact, all over Europe, and in Asia, as well as throughout the American continents, by means of some twenty-odd versions.

There are some beautiful characters, and touching scenes, and wholesome truths in the book, and it is aimed at the reader's very heart, and that from an unsuspected vantage-ground; but it isn't fairly characteristic of the times or the domestic institution of which it treats. Its mistakes are due doubtless to ignorance and passion and not to evil intention. It has mis-statements of fact, law, character, condition and sentiment. In general, the negroes were not abused, but well treated and contented. They cared little for freedom; and not a few of them after their emancipation and some residence in the North, returned to live and die as servants among their own Southern white folks. Mr. George Lunt, an eminent Boston lawyer, in his *Origin of the Late War*, confesses that, – "The negroes were perfectly contented with their lot, and in general they were not only happy in their condition, but proud of it." Even Mrs. Stowe's anti-slavery slave-owner and hero, Mr. Auguste St. Clair, whilst he argues against the institution because of its abuses, says, in answer to the question – "But why didn't you free your own slaves?" *"They were all well satisfied to be as they were."* Already some States had passed laws to restrain and punish negligent and cruel masters. Courts were given power to prevent harsh treatment and the separation by sale of slave families. Many eminent, eloquent and influential Churchmen were advocating the repeal of such laws as forbade the teaching of slaves to read (which laws had been made in self-defense only and to limit somewhat the effect of Abolition books, tracts and papers circulated secretly among our servants.) The Gospel was being everywhere freely preached to them: hundreds of missions were established: multiplied thousands of humble, honest, happy converts had been gathered into the Church of Christ, many planters were building chapels and supporting pastors to minister in spiritual things to their faithful and beloved servants. All these were notable facts, but they have no mention in Mrs. Stowe's famous book: nor has that other undeniable and stupendous fact, that the poor, degraded Southern slave was being so speedily, cheaply, thoroughly and generally trained and qualified for the active and complete citizenship and rulership with which he was to be so soon endowed by Northern power and wisdom, and all this through the conscientious care and personal example and affection of his faithful master and mistress. When the war was ended, the Northern peo-

ple endorsed most fully Sambo's fitness for the ballot and
for Gubernatorial honors and Senatorial seats, but Mrs.
Stowe denies to his quondam teachers their well-earned
meed! Shocking! Shameful!

This Connecticut saint, whilst wilfully ignorant of
the negro himself, and scarcely better informed as to the
domestic system which she sets herself to depict, and as
bitterly prejudiced against the people among whom she
had never lived, but was resolved to represent to all man-
kind, this saint did invent a story of cruelty and crime that
so admirably suited the anti-slavery periodical in which it
was first published and so successfully served the political
party and political purposes for which it was conceived
and issued as to obtain for her a literary immortality.
Some books of fiction are said to be "founded upon fact."
Uncle Tom's Cabin hasn't much foundation of that sort.
It is a mean caricature. It slanders the South. Its characters are angels and demons. Its title should have been –
"The Sins and Sorrows of Our Inter-State Slave Traffic,
Duly Exaggerated and Highly Colored for Political Purposes." Its incidents are quite exceptional, its actors are
overdone, its situations well nigh impossible, its theology
is unscriptural, its conclusions erroneous, its consequences calamitous. I was born in the family of a slave-
owner and grew into manhood in a populous slave State,
and traveled over and resided in the farther South, and yet
I have never seen a slave chased by bloodhounds or
chained or handcuffed or branded or starved or scourged
or sold at auction. I suppose such sights did now and then
happen, but that they truly represent our domestic life, I
deliberately and positively deny.

The evil consequences of *Uncle Tom's Cabin* can
never be fully set forth. If its purpose had been to inflame

human and diabolical passions until all regard for truth, justice, order, law, love, unity, peace and good will should be banished from American breasts – if its object had been to bring into open contempt the laws of the land, the decisions of its highest courts, and the sacred compacts of the Constitution itself – and all these to overthrow the system of domestic servitude in the South – then it was a woeful and wondrous success! The Northern people were wrought into a frenzy; the Southern, in feeling at least, bitterly resented the outrage, and all classes came to realize that the dreaded end was drawing on apace.

Mrs. Stowe spent much time in Florida during her declining years and became more fully acquainted with her brother in black. She found him less desirable than she once thought. An intimate friend of hers is quoted as saying, in her own words, and of her own great book, – "That story had its origin in the brain of a romantic girl, fired by the stories told by my father and my uncle. *I did not know the negro then, or it would never have been written.*" An able editor and devoted friend of the black race, in commenting upon this declaration, sagely remarks – "In the harsh attitude of her old age, when she is said to have reached a point where she would not allow a negro to do anything for her, she was about as far from really knowing the negro as in the romance of her youth." And he is surely correct.

But books and songs and sermons and prayers were all too tame and slow. The popular craze demanded heroic deeds, an inspiring example! This prolonged agitation by Abolition authors and orators caused, several years subsequently, a strange and savage attempt to free the negroes and lead them in a concerted uprising against

their unsuspecting masters. This crazy and wicked effort
was known as the "JOHN BROWN RAID." Brown was a
monomaniac and a murderer from "Bloody Kansas." He
gathered a band of eighteen Northern ruffians, white and
black, and a sum of money furnished by sympathizers in
the North amounting to about $4,000; his store of arms
consisted of two hundred rifles, commonly called "Kansas
Bibles," and "Beecher Bibles" (because bought by his
church); two hundred revolvers, and nine hundred and fifty
long, strong, double-edged blades, fastened on the end of
hoe-handles (made in Ohio) for the use of the negroes who
should join his crusade – they being, of course, unfamiliar
with fire-arms. With this force and outfit, Brown imagined
that he could invade Virginia and overthrow slavery! At
midnight on Sunday, October 16, 1859, he captured Harper's
Ferry, arrested sixty of the chief citizens, seized the United
States Arsenal, and sent forth his conspirators to liberate
the poor down-trodden darkies. Not a negro could be
induced to join the band of emancipation patriots; and one
poor servant was shot for refusing to do so. But the citizens
and troops hastily called out, drove Brown and his followers
into the village engine-house. At the command of the Federal
War Office, Colonel R.E. Lee, who was on furlough, came
from his home at Arlington, took charge of the defense,
and (as is related in his own memorandum) on "Tuesday
about sunrise, with twelve marines under command of
Lieutenant Green (accompanied by Lieutenant J.E.B. Stuart)
broke in the door of the engine-house, secured the robbers
and released the prisoners unhurt. All the conspirators were
killed or mortally wounded but four, John Brown, Aaron
Stevens, Edwin Coppie and Green Shields (black). Had
the prisoners removed to a place of safety and their wounds
dressed."

These brutal and misguided fanatics were given able counsel, a fair trial, a review by the Supreme Court, were convicted of the crime of murder, and hanged – December 2nd, 1859. In the treasonable and murderous assault, five men had been slain and nine wounded, but the legal execution of the felons occasioned a storm of indignation throughout the North. Brown was canonized as *"St. John, the Just,"* and was placed next to our Lord in the catalogue of martyrs. In many Northern cities eloquent eulogies were pronounced, funeral dirges sung, church bells tolled, minute guns fired, and houses and halls draped in deep mourning to express the widespread sympathy for the "martyr who had yielded up his life on the altar of human liberty."

Judge J. S. Black, the great Pennsylvanian, says:

> They applauded John Brown to the echo for a series of the basest murders on record. They did not conceal their hostility to the Federal and State governments, nor deny their enmity to all laws which protected white men. The Constitution stood in their way, and they cursed it bitterly. The Bible was quoted against them, and they reviled God, the Almighty himself.

In its immediate, local, personal effects, Brown's silly and futile assault upon the State of Virginia was scarce worthy of record. No servile war was started. No slave was set free. No "Provisional Government" was established. No "War Department" was organized. No other armed expedition was sent into the field. The red-handed assassin and "Commander-in-Chief," John Brown, was quietly hanged by the Commonwealth of Virginia, as he richly deserved to be for the five murders that he had committed in her borders and for several other cold-blooded deeds done in

Kansas. It was the general and profound feeling excited in the North by his execution that startled the Southern people like a fire bell at night. It was declared in public prints and mass meeting addresses that the death of the "New Saint will make the gallows glorious like the Cross." Such language from Ralph Waldo Emerson, applauded by the culture and conscience of a multitude in Boston, admonished the South in tones and terms unmistakable that "the irrepressible conflict" foretold the year before by the leader and idol of the party, W. H. Seward (later Lincoln's Secretary of State), was now on. No man could doubt now that our "House was divided against itself." The whole world was advertised that, "the Union could not permanently endure half slave and half free." And these public demonstrations and inflammatory speeches mightily aided in causing that prediction of Lincoln to come to pass. As evidence and illustration of the State of the public mind at the North, at this time, take the testimony of an intelligent and representative man who was then studying his profession in their midst. He gives this short statement of his experience: –

> I myself saw the demonstrations of the Northern people on that occasion, happening at that time to be living in Philadelphia. It was instantly plain to me that I was in an enemy's country. The Southern students around me saw it as plainly as I did. It took but a dozen sentences to open the eyes of the least intelligent. It was only to say – "Come on boys, let's go," and three hundred of us marched over on our own side of the line.

It must have been a clear case, and a very strong feeling, that induced these three hundred bright, best men from Dixie to abandon their lecture-rooms and turn their backs on professional honors, and follow Dr. Hunter McGuire to the Southland to escape from it. It was *that feeling* – wide spread and ever deepening – that brought on the war, *not* "property" in negroes. The seeds of Abolitionism sown so diligently for thirty years had ripened at last, and the harvest must be reaped. It was evident that, – "In the North, there is a higher law than the Constitution which regulates our authority over the domain. Slavery must be abolished and we must do it. The times demand, and we must have, an anti-slavery Constitution, an anti-slavery Bible, and an anti-slavery God!" That was their slogan!

This declaration of principles and purposes had been strikingly summarized and exemplified as far back as 1844, by "The American Anti-Slavery Society," which boldly cast aside the Constitution and denounced it as "a covenant with death, and an agreement with hell." In full accord with this view, and faithfully reflecting this feeling, many Northern governors refused to give up upon legal requisition the fugitive slaves hidden in their States' borders, and Federal marshals were often mobbed for arresting runaways in Northern cities, whilst fourteen State Legislatures "nullified" the Constitution by passing "personal liberty laws." It availed nothing that these "laws" were declared to be unconstitutional again and again by the highest Federal courts, and by the Supreme Court of the United States. Passion ruled, not law. The Supreme Court of the United States also decided that under the Constitution, we might move into the territories and be protected with our property, but Lincoln said, that "he didn't care what the Supreme Court decided he would turn us out anyhow" – and yet in the Hampton-Roads Conference (1865), he admitted that, "The people of the

North were as responsible for slavery as the people of the South." In one single State (New York), in one single year, 1850, one single Abolition society aided to escape from their lawful owners one hundred and fifty-one fugitives. On May 1st of that year, Chairman Garritt Smith had this report of work done read in open session in New York City, remarking – "For that, you know, is our business." By such means, from 1810 to 1861, it is estimated by Chief Justice Taney of Maryland, that $28,500,000 worth of negroes were enticed to leave their lawful owners. It was thus that my own "Black Mammy" was lured from the parsonage in Covington, Kentucky, whilst I had yet much need of her!

There was another cause that contributed powerfully to produce the discontent which at last resulted in disunion – a cause as provoking as any that has been named – a cause far older than the Harriet Beecher Stowe book, and yet as recent as the John Brown raid, and even more costly to the South – a cause of more widespread influence, if not of so sudden and shocking effects, than of both those combined – the enactment by Congress of PROTECTIVE TARIFF LAWS. For years unnumbered, these had been the means of financial and commercial disparagement and depletion of the South. The Federal Constitution conferred upon Congress the power "to lay and collect Taxes, Duties, Imposts and Excises to pay the Debts and provide for the common Defense and general Welfare of the United States." Under this authority, in the year 1816, duties unjust and oppressive to the South, were first made legal, and such are being still collected. The system had its origin in a benevolent design to provide for the debt left upon us by the War of 1812, and also to indemnify certain Northern patriots for services rendered and losses sustained during and after that successful struggle. These New England mechanics and merchants had invested capital in manufacturing plants and war materials which the welcome but unexpected peace had rendered of little further use and much diminished value. The consequent fall in prices of such goods threatened these citizens with heavy losses, and it was to prevent greater depreciation of values that the tariff of 1816 was proposed and enacted. At the outset, the motive was sympathetic and patriotic; in the progress of commerce and legislation, it became selfish and sectional; and in the end, the effort brought on a bloody, wicked and fratricidal war. To this day, it has operated to enrich immensely the Northern States, and as steadily to reduce the South. As President Davis says – "It presented the not uncommon occurrence of a good case making a bad precedent." Well, the mischievous precedent has been faithfully followed and a blind man might now see in the ever-increasing vigor of the system its destined immortality. *Why not?* The North man loves money and has the votes!

The whole history of tariff legislation is a striking illustration of that memorable saying of the great Kansas jurist, Justice Miller – "Of all the powers conferred upon Government, that of taxation is the most liable to abuse." A Southern man can scarcely help adding that, of all the abuses of power ever exercised in making law in our great Republic, the most odious and hurtful to the South has been that used to fasten upon us those duties which give to individual business and sectional interests high protection at the expense of the general public and the general good.

In our early years – from 1789 to 1816 – import duties gave, of course, some incidental protection, yet Mr.

82

rcan, and had for its father Mr. Clay of
Kentucky, but the Confederate Admiral Raphael Semmes
has, with far finer descriptive discrimination and much
better perspective view, styled it "the *System of Spoliation.*" The underlying patriotic impulse of the statesmen
of that day was to foster, for a time, certain "infant industries," and not to inaugurate for centuries a scheme of
taxation that should rob one section of our country to
adorn, enrich and strengthen the other. The sin and shame
of the latter-day politicians is, by it, to shut out all foreign
goods from our home markets and thus enable the Northern manufacturer to sell us his own wares at his own
prices. Nobody can call him unnatural, but his policy can
hardly be regarded as patriotic or tending to bind us more
closely to him. And the framers of the Constitution never
contemplated such a perversion of its powers. Had it been
foreseen, the Article allowing it would never have been
adopted.

The North had many and deep harbors, fleets of
boats and ships, capable and hungry-seamen, immense
and cheap water-power, much invested capital, thousands
of skilled workmen and inventive mechanics. She needed
only the Southern raw materials at the lowest prices, and
that we should buy her manufactured goods at the highest
figures, and she would become rich and strong – no
matter what the South should say or do. The result has
not disappointed her. But the long lane may have its
"turn!" "The mills of the gods grind slowly, but they grind

exceeding fine."

The South, although always agricultural, was always ready to favor tariffs for revenue, and it was only when duties were so laid as to pay bounties, subsidies, and promote private gain and sectional glory, that she resisted, and resisted in vain. The majority ruled. One such bill was under consideration in 1828, called "the Bill of Abominations," when Mr. Drayton, of South Carolina, moved that the title be amended to read – "An Act to increase the duties upon certain imports for the purpose of increasing the profits of certain manufacturers;" his object being to bring, in this way, the validity of the law to the test of the Supreme Court of the United States. His motion was defeated, of course. The tariff lords wanted no judicial decision upon their scheme for pecuniary gain and sectional aggrandizement. The bill was so wisely worded as to pass for a revenue measure, and thus to escape possible legal examination, while it was in reality a scheme for protection. Is it to be wondered at that a sovereign State should bethink herself of "nullification" as a remedy, when no other was left her? Isn't self-preservation a right of Sovereignty as well as a law of Nature?

It has been often asserted by Northern politicians that the South favored these tariff rates until 1828, but the records of Congress show the charge to be untrue. The memorials for them came from the North; the speeches made against them were all from the South. The votes for them were almost all from the North. In 1818, eight Northern States supported it. The six Southern States were strongly against it. In 1824, only Massachusetts and New Hampshire voted against it. While the two Carolinas, Georgia, Alabama, Mississippi and Louisiana were unanimously opposed to it. So, too, "in 1842, the South

was largely against the protective act of that year." Had
the case been otherwise, the South would not have cut out
of the Confederate Constitution the "General Welfare"
clause, which had been for fifty years the stronghold of the
protectionists; nor would she have prohibited all "Bounties
from her Treasury, and all Duties on Importations from
foreign nations, to promote or foster any branch of
industry." Such facts refute ten thousands of misrepresentations. Indeed, her whole history in the Union, and her
experience under the system disprove the falsehood.

Senator Benton, of Missouri, although no friend
of slavery, gave in the United States Senate, in 1828, this
double reason for the persistent opposition of the South
to such ruinous legislation –

> I feel for the sad changes that have taken place
> in the South during the last fifty years. Before the
> Revolution, it was the seat of wealth as well as of
> hospitality. Money, and all it commanded, abounded
> there. But how now? All this is reversed. Wealth has
> fled from the South and settled in the regions North of
> the Potomac. And this in the face of the fact that the
> South, in four staples alone, has exported produce since
> the revolution, to the value of eight hundred millions of
> dollars; and the North has exported comparatively
> nothing. Such an export would indicate unparalleled
> wealth, but what is the fact? In the place of wealth, a
> universal pressure for money was felt – not enough for
> current expenses – the price of all property down – the
> country drooping and languishing – towns and cities
> decaying – and the frugal habits of the people pushed to
> the verge of universal self-denial for the preservation of
> their family estates. Such a result is a strange and
> wonderful phenomenon. It calls upon statesmen to
> inquire into the cause. Under Federal legislation the ex-

ports of the South have been the basis of the Federal revenue. . . . Virginia, the two Carolinas, and Georgia, may be said to defray three-fourths of the annual expenses of supporting the Federal Government; and of this great sum, annually furnished by them, nothing, or next to nothing, is returned to them in the shape of Government expenditures. That expenditure flows in an opposite direction. It flows northwardly in one uniform, uninterrupted, and perennial stream. This is the reason why wealth disappears from the South, and rises up in the North. Federal legislation does all this. It does it by the simple process of taking eternally from the South and returning nothing to it. If it returned to the South the whole, or even a good part of what it exacted, the four States south of the Potomac might stand the action of the system, but the South must be exhausted of its money and property by a course of legislation which is forever taking away and never returning anything. Every new tariff increases the force of this action. No tariff has ever yet included Virginia, the two Carolinas, and Georgia, except to increase the burdens imposed upon them.

This double back-action principle for keeping poor the South is, like the poor themselves, always with us, and there seems no help for us.

Dr. Albert Taylor Bledsoe, referring to the question raised by Senator Benton, says: –

How did slavery produce this wonderful transformation? How did slavery work all this ruin? Slavery, it is well known, existed before the Revolution as well as afterward; and accompanied the South in the palmiest days of her prosperity, as well as in the darkest and most dismal hour of her adversity. Hence, it was not, and could not have been, the one cause of so great and so sudden a change. And besides, instead of having ceased to produce, the fair and fruitful South continued to pour forth, in greater abundance than ever, the broad streams of national prosperity and wealth. Hence she was impoverished, not because the fountains of her former supply had been dried up, or even diminished in volume, but because the great streams flowing from them did not return into her own bosom. Into what region of the earth then, did these streams empty themselves?

Let every landscape, harbor, sea coast, mountain side, lake front, and city park, stately corner, and public highway, decorated and protected by Federal treasury funds answer it. And if any tourist wonders at the startling contrast seen throughout the Sunny South, let him be told in tones of hypocritical pity, "Ah! *You behold here the blight of slavery.* The thrift that you saw in the North was due to the invigorating, glorious air of freedom! What a sad thing it is that the South was so long cursed with slavery!" Comrades, don't that make you weary and feel the need of prayer?

But it wasn't freedom alone that adorned, strengthened, enriched, peopled and glorified the North. The almighty dollar played its part. Yankee Doodle wanted many things – wider roads, higher bridges, bigger tunnels, deeper harbors, longer canals, additional light-houses, more buoys, locks, docks, dams, forts, arsenals, smoother highways, safer travel, cheaper transportation, easier post-routes, handsomer cities, parks, historical gates, groups, arches, monuments, statues, and the like; and as votes make the laws, and the laws make money, and money makes every improvement, why should she not have all the improvements that heart can wish, and money buy? Have them, she will! The South – well – she may have as Dr. Bledsoe says – "The crumbs that fall from the rich man's table!"

The South took up arms not to extend slave territory, not alone to keep the blacks in bondage, not for the balance of power, not for commercial supremacy, not to destroy the Union, but to maintain her political rights, especially the *original, inherent, sovereign, blood-bought right of local self-government* – to escape the centralization of power in the Federal Government which was now determined to reduce the Southern States to a condition of political helplessness. The North tried to load down the South with the odium of slavery as the cause of secession and war, but it was only the circumstance that brought on the explosion, the fuse that fired the magazine; the dynamite was deep hidden in the political doctrines of the sections which were diametrically opposed and antagonistic. General Lee must have known for what he fought, and he writes of the war as *"our struggle for State rights and Constitutional government."* Would Lee be ignorant of it or lie about it? After the overthrow of General McClellan in the "Seven Days Battles," in front of Richmond, the Confederate Chief in an address of congratulation to his victorious army, refers to their humane treatment of their (ten thousand) prisoners, as "the fit crowning glory to your valor," and then in a single line, speaking for himself and all Southern soldiers, says, *"you are fighting for all that is dearest to man."* Did he mean the negroes that the Yankees had unloaded on us? Who can think it?

General Order No. 16, To the Army of Northern Virginia, was issued July 11th, 1863, just a week after the fight at Gettysburg. I suppose by that time General Lee had learned for what he was fighting. It runs – "Let every soldier remember that on his courage and fidelity depends all that makes life worth having, the freedom of his country, the honor of his people, and the security of his home. Soldiers, your old enemy is before you. Win from him honor worthy of your cause, worthy of your comrades dead on so many illustrious fields." Was Lee ignorant of the objects of the war, or was he unable to state them?

The responsibility of the North for the war is avouched by Abraham Lincoln himself. "It is you, Medill, (of the *Chicago Tribune*), who is largely responsible for making blood flow as it has. You called for war until you had it. I have given it to you. What you have asked for you have had. Now you come begging to be let off from the call for more men, which I have made to carry on the war that you demanded. You ought to be ashamed of yourself!" So says Miss Tarbell in *Lincoln's Life. Query,* If Medill is responsible, how can Davis and Toombs be?

The immediate cause of the war, the act that brought on the trouble was an attempt by the Federal administration to reinforce and provision Fort Sumter. This fort, commanding the harbor, was within the domain of South Carolina. The State had withdrawn from the Union by the formal and unanimous action of her people in Convention assembled. The fort was held by soldiers of the United States. These were expecting reinforcements. A fleet with arms and provisions was waiting in the near-by waters. Eleven ships carrying twenty-six guns and two thousand four hundred men from the North had gone to strengthen the garrison "peaceably if permitted, forcibly if they must." *That* "overt act" began the war! The firing of Beauregard was merely the natural consequence. The Southron *fired* first, the Northman had *drawn* first. Our shot was in self defense, to prevent being taken in front and rear. The only question arising is, was Beauregard under obligation to wait for his foe to strike him down –

was not the armed attitude and hostile intention of his enemy ample provocation to justify "the shot that was heard around the world?" The people of Dixie think it was. But let us look more closely into the question.

On February 18, 1861, Jefferson Davis and Alexander H. Stevens were inaugurated President and Vice-President. Mr. Davis at once named his cabinet and complied with the convention's instructions, "to send duly accredited commissioners to Washington to establish *friendly* relations and to adjust all matters of public property, public debt, etc., so as to *avoid* war, and upon principles of right, justice, equity and good faith" – so read their credentials. Previously, and at once upon her secession. South Carolina had sent commissioners for the same purpose. Their special mission had been to treat for Forts Moultrie and Sumter in Charleston Harbor, and which, ceded by South Carolina to the Government, in trust, and for the defense of Charleston, by law, reverted to the State upon her secession. Sumter was then unoccupied and Major Robert Anderson with sixty-three men, lay in Fort Moultrie. Before these commissioners could see President Buchanan, Major Anderson, acting under orders, spiked his guns in Moultrie, and by night moved his garrison to Sumter, which with stronger walls and surrounded by water was more easily held. (This was itself a warlike act, in a time of peace, and done by "night," too.) After one fruitless interview with the President, who declined to receive them or their communications, the commissioners returned home, having effected nothing. The appointment and instructions of these two commissions clearly indicates the peaceable intentions of the South. Further proof is found also in the early and earnest efforts of Virginia to promote "pacific settlement" by inviting all the States to a Peace Congress to meet in Washington, February 4, 1861. Twenty-one States responded, but it all ended, to quote Senator Chandler, of Michigan – "In thin smoke." That gentleman was strongly opposed to any compromise, had urged his State "to send stiff-backed men or none," and argued that "without a little blood-letting, this Union will not be worth a rush."

That the South did not desire or expect war is further apparent from her defenseless condition. She had no army and no weapons, nor was there a powder mill, or rifle factory in all the seceding States, so that afterwards, some regiments were armed with pikes only, and others with flint-locks and shot guns! Many thought that sober and wiser counsels would prevail in the North; so that the States might soon return to the Union; others felt that the separation was permanent, but would be peaceable; only rabid extremists talked of war. In the North as well, there was no thought of battle or bloodshed. From the platform, through the press, in great centers, in Congress, and even by the President, the opinion had been widely and strongly expressed that a war of coercion was unconstitutional, unjust and impossible.

The question of coercion had long ago been incidentally passed upon and legally settled by the highest court known to our political system. In the contest over rendition between Ohio and Kentucky, being tried by the United States Supreme Court, speaking of the powers held respectively by State and Federal Governments, Mr. Chief Justice Taney, in giving the Court's decision said: "While admitting that the Constitution is mandatory on the Governors, there is not a line in it which gives power to the General Government to compel a State to do anything." This opinion was as widely accepted as it was judicially well founded.

The fact is that, so far from possessing or even claiming to possess, "The power to compel a State" to remain in the Union, our General Government had held all along, and had for many years actually *taught the doctrine of the lawfulness of secession.* This fact has been clearly established by many competent witnesses. Large credit for the knowledge of it is due to Col. Robert Bingham, superintendent of Bingham School, Asheville, North Carolina. By recent painstaking, and persevering correspondence, he has proven quite fully that, since 1825 and probably to 1840, Rawle's *View of the Constitution of the United States* was a text-book in the Military Academy at West Point, where the future commanders of the armies of the Republic are thoroughly instructed in both the science and art of warfare. This evidence I will give in part here, for the sake of the light it throws upon the question of the right of peaceful secession, as well as on the matter of the guilt or innocency of the crimes of treason and rebellion in the conduct of the greatest soldiers in the armies of the Southern Confederacy. Having Rawle's work in my own library, I can certify to the correctness of the quotations given below. But first of the author, book, students, etc. Hear these witnesses.

(From the Superintendent of the
United States Military Academy.)

Headquarters United States Military Academy,
West Point, N. Y.
Nov. 18, 1904.
* * * In the forthcoming Memorial Volume of the Military Academy now being printed will appear the following note regarding the book:

342, 731 R., 20 Rawle (William): "A View of the Constitution of the United States of America." Philadelphia, 1825, 1v., O.

The text-book, of the law department from — to —. The copy of this book owned by Library, United States Military Academy makes it very probable that it was used as a text book.

(Signed) A.L. MILLS, BRIG.-GEN., U.S.A., *Superintendent.*

(From the Librarian of the United States Military Academy.)

Library, United States Military Academy, West Point, N.Y., Nov. 23, 1904.

* * * The copy of Rawle (William): "A View of the Constitution of the United States of America;" Philadelphia, 1825; 1v., O., owned by the Library, U.S.M.A., contains Ms. notes which make it *very probable* that this book was used as a text-book at the Military Academy, inasmuch as there is a list of sections and lessons marked. The book contains no information as to just the period during which it was used as a text-book, nor have we been able to find this out up to the present time.

(Signed) EDWARD S. HOLDEN, *Librarian,*

(From the Librarian of Congress).

Library of Congress, Washington, Dec. 3, 1904.

* * * I find on examination of the Annual Catalogues of the West Point Military Academy that no text-books appear to be named until A.D., 1842.

(Signed) A.R. SPOFFORD.

(From a Great-grandson of Wm. Rawle).

211 S. Sixth Street,
Philadelphia, Dec. 13, 1904.

* * * The book entitled, "A View of the Constitution of the United States of America" was written by my great grandfather. * * * The book was, I think, the first by the author, after having studied law in New York under the Royul Attorney General and later in the Middle Temple in London, was admitted to the Philadelphia bar, September 15, 1783. He was therefore of an age to appreciate the doings of the Constitutional Convention of 1787, which sat in this City where he resided. Doubtless he attended its sittings, although I do not find among his papers any statement to that effect. The work, I have always understood, was for many years used as a text-book at the United States Military Academy at West Point.

(Signed) WM. BROOKE RAWLE.

(From John Rawle, Grandson of Wm. Rawle).

Natchez, Miss., Jan. 27, 1905.

* * * In re, William Rawle, my grandfather, I am aware that his view on the "Constitution of the United States" was used as a text-book at West Point, but I do not recollect in what years it was. Gen. R. E. Lee, et al., said that they were taught by that book while at West Point. * * * General Lee told Bishop Wilmer, of Louisiana, that if it had not been for the instruction he got from Rawle's text-book at West Point he would not have left the Old Army and joined the South at the breaking out of the late war between the States.

(Signed) JOHN RAWLE.

(From Joseph Wilmer, a Son of Bishop Wilmer).

Rapidan, Va., Feb. 10, 1905.
* * * I have a distinct recollection of my father's statement that Greneral Lee told him that "Rawle" was a text-book during his cadetship at West Point. * * *

(From Mrs. M. J. Leeds, Granddaughter
of William Rawle).

New Orleans, La., Jan. 19, 1905.
* * * I am positive that the work of my grandfather, William Rawle, was used as a text-book at West Point. I have heard this from my own father, Judge Edward Rawle, who died in 1880, a son of the author of the book.
(Signed) MRS. M. J. LEEDS.

(From Judge G. L. Christian).

Christian & Christian Law Offices,
Chamber of Commerce Building
Richmond, Va., Dec. 1904
* * * I have frequently heard Generals D. H. Maury and Fitzhugh Lee state the fact that "Rawle on the Constitution" was one of the text-books used at West Point when they were students there. I have also heard the same statement iterated and reiterated time and time again without any suggestion that there was any question about it. I saw General Lee last night, and he again told me that there was no doubt about this being the fact.
(Signed) GEO. L. CHRISTIAN.

(From General Fitzhugh Lee)

Norfolk, Va., Dec. 5, 1904.

* * * My recollection is that Rawle's *View of the Constitution* was the legal text-book at West Point when Generals Lee, Joseph E. Johnson and Stonewall Jackson were cadets there, and later on was a text-book when I was a cadet there.

(Signed) FITZHUGH LEE.

(From General Dabney H. Maury).

In Vol. 6, p. 249, *So. Historical Papers*:

* * * It (Rawle) remained as a text-book at West Point till — ; and Mr. Davis and Sidney Johnston and General Joe Johnston and General Lee and all the rest of us who retired with Virginia from the Federal Union, were not only obeying the plain instincts of our nature and dictates of duty, but we were obeying the very inculcations we had received in the National Schools. It is not probable that any of us ever read the Constitution or any exposition of it except this work of Rawle, which we studied in our Graduating year at West Point. I know I did not. * * *

(Signed) DABNEY H. MAURY.

(From Charles Francis Adams.)

Adams Building, 23 Court Street
Boston, Dec. 8, 1904.

* * * Herewith, under another cover, I send a copy of a publication of mine (*The Constitutional Ethics of Secession*), which bears very directly upon the point made in your letter. On page 16, in Note 1, may be found all I know on the subject of Rawle's *View of the Constitution*, and the use of its as a text-book at West Point.

You will note I there state as a fact that his

View was the text-book in use at West Point prior to
1840. * * * I remember that, at that time (two years ago)
I looked the matter up with the utmost care, correspond-
ing with the librarian and authorities at West Point, and
also with at least one legal authority in New York. The
result and my conclusion, are set forth in the note.

(Signed) CHAS. F. ADAMS.

From *The Constitutional Ethics of Secession*,
by Chas. Francis Adams. Houghton, Mifflin & Co.,
Boston, 1903, pages 16–17:

(1) Much has been written and said, and still
more declaimed, as to the peculiar and exceptional allegiance due, in case of attempted secession, to the National Government on the part of the graduates of the
Military Academy at West Point. It is, however, a no-
ticeable fact that anterior to 1840 the doctrine of the
right of secession seems to have been inculcated at West
Point as an admitted principle of Constitutional Law!
Story's *Commentaries* was first published in 1833.
Prior to its appearance the standard text-book on the
subject was Rawle's *View of the Constitution*. This was
published in Philadelphia in 1825. William Rawle, its
author, was an eminent Philadelphia lawyer. A man of
twenty-nine at the time the Constitution was adopted,
and already in active professional life; in 1792 he was
offered a judicial position by Washington. Subsequently
he was for many years Chancellor of the Law Associa-
tion of Philadelphia, and principal author of the revised
code of Pennsylvania. He stood in the foremost rank of
the legal luminaries of the first third of the century. His
instincts, sympathies and connections were all national.
Prior to 1840, his *View* was the text-book in use at West
Point.

From *The Republic of Republics.*
Little, Brown & Co., Boston,
4th Edition, 1878, Preface, p. V:

Another event of great historical interest in which Judge Clifford participated, was a solemn consultation of a small number of the ablest lawyers of the North in Washington a few months after the war upon the momentous question as to whether the Federal Government should commence a criminal prosecution against Jefferson Davis for his participation and leadership in the war of secession. In this council, which was surrounded at the time with the utmost secrecy, were Attorney-General Speed, Judge Clifford, Wm. Evarts, and perhaps half a dozen others, who had been selected from the whole Northern profession for their legal ability and acumen, and the result of their deliberation was the sudden abandonment (of the idea of a prosecution) in view of the insurmountable difficulties in the way of getting a final conviction.

Republic of Republics, page 44:

The above work (Rawle's *View*) was a textbook at West Point when Lee and Davis were cadets there.

Footnote 1, p. 33:

They (Davis and Lee) were at West Point during the administration of John Quincy Adams, who, as late as 1839, essayed to teach the whole American people that, "the people of each State have a right to secede from the confederated Union." These are his very words.

The Republics of Republics is understood to have given some of the lines of defense by Jefferson Davis' counsel if the case had been brought to trial, and to have had the approval of Mr. Davis himself. The book is very highly spoken of by Charles O'Connor, one of Mr. Davis' counsel, and one of the most distinguished lawyers in the United States in his day, who wrote to the author in 1865 (see page IV), * * * "with so admirably prepared and so overwhelmingly conclusive a brief (as his book) my task (of defending Mr. Davis) would be easy indeed."

If there were "insurmountable difficulties in the way of getting a final conviction," it stands to reason that, the defense "would be easy, indeed."

The following letter explains itself:

> 4117 Pine Street,
> Philadelphia, March 25, 1884.
>
> Dear Col. Bingham: While the question of Jeff. Davis's trial for high treason was pending, Mr. Wm. B. Reed, counsel for the defense, was a member of my brother's congregation at Orange Valley, N.J. He told my brother, after it had been decided that the trial was not to take place, that if the case had come to trial the defense would have offered in evidence the text-book on constitutional law (Rawle's *View of the Constitution*) from which Davis had been instructed at West Point by the authority of the United States Government, and in which the right of secession is maintained as one of the constitutional rights of a State. You are quite at liberty to refer to me for this statement, which is given according to the best of my recollection.
>
> L. W. BACON.

This cloud of witnesses, living and dead, men and women, Northern and Southern, military and literary, establishes satisfactorily at least nine points; namely: 1st – That Wm. Rawle did write and publish in 1825, in Philadelphia, *A View of the Constitution.* 2d – That he was a very able man, thoroughly competent, and favorably situated to execute his task. 3rd – That his book does teach the right of secession. 4th – That it was an accepted authority in that day. 5th – That it was a text-book in the course at West Point, where it remains still, and yet showing the class-lesson marks. 6th – That General Lee was then, and for years afterwards there as cadet and student. 7th – That in 1861, he defended the cause of Virginia and the South rather than fight for "the Union," and this because of the instruction given him at West Point. 8th – That the Federal Government knowing these facts, and that they would be brought out by counsel in court if President Davis should be put upon trial for treason, decided not to try him, thus denying him the opportunity to vindicate himself and his co-patriots of the Southland. 9th – That Lee himself said that he would not have left the old Army and joined the South, but for the instruction that he had received from Rawle's *View of the Constitution.*

In the face of these facts how monstrous would have been the attempt to punish for treason Mr. Davis or General Lee, who had only put into practice the doctrine taught them at West Point! And how cruel to accuse President Davis of it, imprison and indict him for it, and then deny him a hearing in which he might prove himself innocent! How would such a record as this have looked on the page of History? Cadet Jefferson Davis is taught at West Point in 1825 the lawfulness of secession. The said Davis practices in 1861 the said doctrine with the people of Mississippi. The United States Government charges with treason the said Davis, and tries him at Richmond, Virginia, in 1866 for doing what it had taught him was lawful when he was at West Point. And the said Davis was acquitted for the sole reason that the jury could *"find no fault in him"*?

The extracts from Rawle's *View* need no preface or explanation. He says:

> If a faction should attempt to subvert the government of a State for the purpose of destroying its republican form, the national power of the Union could be called forth to subdue it. Yet it is not to be understood that its interposition would be justifiable if a State should determine to retire from the Union (p. 289).
>
> It depends on the State itself whether it will continue a member of the Union. To deny this right would be inconsistent with the principle on which all our political systems are founded, which is, that the people have in all cases the right to determine how they shall be governed (p. 289).
>
> The States may then wholly withdraw from the Union (p. 290).
>
> We have associated as republics. Possessing the power to form monarchies, republics were preferred and instituted.
>
> If a majority of the people of a State deliberately and peaceably resolve to relinquish the republican form of government, they cease to be members of the Union (p. 292).
>
> The secession of a State from the Union depends on the will of the people of such State (p. 295).
>
> In any manner by which secession is to take place, nothing is more certain than that the act should be deliberate, clear and unequivocal (p. 296).
>
> The people of a State may have reason to complain in respect to the acts of the general government; they may, in such cases, invest some of their own officers with the power of negotiation, and may declare an

absolute secession in case of failure. The secession in such cases must be distinctly and peremptorily declared to take place, and in such case, as the case of unconditional secession, the previous ligament with the Union would be legitimately and fairly destroyed (p. 296).

It was foreseen that there would be a natural tendency to increase the number of the States. It was also known that a State might withdraw itself (p. 297).

Secessions may reduce the number of the States to the smallest integer admitting combination.

To withdraw from the Union is a solemn, serious act.

Whenever it may appear expedient to the people of a State to withdraw from the Union, it must be manifested in a direct and unequivocal manner (p. 298).

And also this right (of secession) must be considered an ingredient in the original composition of the general government, and the doctrine heretofore presented in regard to the indefeasible nature of personal allegiance is so far qualified in respect to allegiance to the United States. It was observed that the reciprocal relations of protection and allegiance might cease in certain events, and it was further observed that allegiance would necessarily cease in case of the dissolution of the society (the Union in that case) to which it was due (p. 289–290).

But I was speaking of the collision at Sumter. This changed things and precipitated the struggle. For this, the South has been universally blamed, but *the facts are these:* – The fort belonged to the Federal Government, was built and held in trust for the defense of Charleston; the site belonged to South Carolina and had been ceded in trust to the Government on condition that it should be used for that purpose. When the secession of the State put that defense out of the question, commissioners were sent, as we have seen, to treat for the transfer of the fort. They were repulsed. As soon as the Confederacy was established, another commission was sent to adjust these property rights and treat for the transfer of Sumter, the only fort yet held by the United States Government. Mr. Lincoln had been inaugurated meanwhile and the commissioners had to deal with his Secretary of State, Mr. W. H. Seward. Negotiations were conducted through Justices Nelson and Campbell of the Supreme Court of the United States, because Mr. Seward declined to see the commissioners himself. Nelson urged Seward to refrain from any policy of coercion, on the ground that such "is serious violation of the Constitution." On March 15, Mr. Seward authorized Judge Campbell in writing to tell Mr. Davis that "Before a letter could reach him, he would learn by telegraph that the order for evacuation of Sumter had been made." This word was sent. March 20th, Campbell again saw Seward, who told him that *"The delay in the evacuation of the fort was accidental,"* and repeated his assurance that the garrison would be withdrawn. Campbell says, "I repeated this assurance in writing to the commissioners, and informed Mr. Seward in writing, what I had said to them." March 19th, the day *before* this renewed assurance was given, a special envoy had left Washington for Charleston to obtain information and devise means by which Sumter might be – *not evacuated, but reinforced!* And Mr. George Lunt of Massachusetts says – "It was intended to draw the fire of the Confederates" – a silent aggression to produce an active aggression.

Pledging "pacific purposes," Captain G. V. Fox, sent from Washington by Lincoln, was allowed by Governor Pickens to visit the fort, where on the parapet, at night, of March 21st, he had a private interview with Major Anderson, matured his plan, submitted, and had it approved by President Lincoln, and was sent to New York to arrange for its execution. Anderson strongly opposed the attempt to reinforce him: he "at once earnestly condemned it" – so says Major General S. W. Crawford, U.S. Army – "said it was too late; agreed with his superior. General Scott, that an entrance by sea was impossible, and said that the coming of reinforcements would bring on a collision and inaugurate a civil war, and to this he manifested the most earnest opposition." The belief was now general on both sides that the garrison would be withdrawn, and Major Anderson had given his official instructions as to the disposal of the property. (See *The Genesis of Civil War*, by Crawford.)

On March 25th, Col. Ward H. Lamon, another envoy, sent by Lincoln, "informed me," says Governor Pickens, that he had come as confidential agent of the President *"to arrange for the removal of the garrison."* After a visit to the fort, and his return to Washington, he wrote the Governor that he "hoped to return in a few days to withdraw the command." This was on March 30th, fifteen days after Mr. Seward's original assurance of evacuation, and ten days after his explanation that the delay in doing it was "accidental." On April 1st, Campbell again saw Seward, who gave him the statement in writing for the Commissioners – "The Government will not undertake to supply Sumter without notice to Governor Pickens." As this assurance was very different from the others, Campbell asked him, "Whether I was to understand that there had been a change in his former communications?" Seward answered, *"None."* On April 7th, in view of continued rumors of hostile preparations of the Government, Campbell again wrote Seward, asking whether "the assurances given were well or ill founded?" Seward wrote back – *"Faith as to Sumter fully kept. Wait and see."* Yet the day *before* this, Mr. Lincoln had sent one of Seward's officials, a Mr. Chew of the State Department, to notify Governor Pickens that "An attempt will be made to supply Sumter with provisions only, but no attempt will be made to throw in men, arms or ammunition." And yet, in spite of this promise, and against the protest of several cabinet officers, of the Commander-in-Chief of the army, and of Major Anderson himself, a squadron of eleven vessels with twenty-six guns and 2,400 men had been ordered by Lincoln to be ready to sail on April the sixth and appeared off the mouth of Charleston Harbor on April 11th, but was prevented from entering by a storm. The news of the coming fleet having reached the Confederate Government, it sought to obtain possession of Sumter before the reinforcements reached it, and April 11th was spent in dispatches between Major Anderson and General Beauregard, in which the latter asked the evacuation of the fort, and offered every facility for the removal of men, and arms and property. The former regretted that "sense of honor, and of obligation to my Government, prevents compliance," and sent thanks for what he calls "the fair, manly, courteous terms proposed and for the high compliment to me." April 12th, expecting the fleet any moment to enter the Harbor, Beauregard sent word to Anderson that he would open fire. Thus the South fired the first gun. The student of the above facts will judge for himself, who began the war, and whether or not it was treason and rebellion or necessary self-defense. Hallam, the great English Historian, says – "The aggressor in war, that is, he who begins it, is not the first who uses force, but the first who renders force necessary."

To aid my hearer's judgment, and to vindicate my countrymen now gone to the bar of God, I here recite one additional fact as evidence, from the lips of a witness never impeached, and upon authority that will not be questioned. In his *Life of Lee*, Dr. H. A. White of the Washington and Lee University, notes the fact that, "an ordinance of secession submitted to the Virginia Convention, March 17th, was rejected by a vote of ninety to forty-five." Just two to one against it. The new President, the successor in the seat of Washington, requested at once an interview with some representative of the Convention. On April 4th, Mr. J. B. Baldwin, President of the Convention, and who had voted against the secession of Virginia, on March 17th, was sent to Washington and had a conference with Lincoln. He was greeted by the President with the assertion that he had come *too late*. So he has stated under oath. Lincoln would not listen to his pleadings that he should yield the Southern forts, and so preserve peace. Now remember this – On April 4th, Lincoln declares – *"It is too late."* But on April 7th, his Secretary of State, Seward being urged in writing by Judge Campbell to say whether the assurances so often given the Commissioners were well or ill founded (as to the removal of the garrison from Sumter), replied in writing – "Faith as to Sumter fully kept. Wait and see." The question is, who told the truth? Light is thrown on it by other undeniable statements and facts of record. The next day, an official note, unsigned and undated, was handed Governor Pickens in Charleston, South Carolina, by Mr. Chew, of the State Department at Washington, who said

that it was from Lincoln, and had been given to him by
the President of the United States, on April 6th, or only
a day *before* the assurance of Seward that, as to Sumter,
"faith would be fully kept." The paper said – "I am di-
rected by the President of the United States to notify you
to expect an attempt will be made to supply Fort Sumter
with provisions only: and that, if such an attempt be not
resisted, no effort to throw in men, arms or ammunition
will be made without further notice, or in case of an attack upon the fort." This shows clearly that Lincoln told
the truth to Mr. Baldwin on April 4th in saying that "It is
too late." He had already ordered the invasion of
Charleston harbor by armed men and ships.

Here is disclosed a scheme to gain time by mis-
leading the Confederates until an armed fleet fully
provisioned could be sent into the Charleston Harbor to
supply and reinforce the little garrison. The President
played his part, and the Secretary played his, and one
seems about as honest and honorable as the other. But,
my hearer, "wait and see!" On the 12th of April, a second
Committee was sent from Richmond to see the President,
and ascertain definitely his policy. On the 14th day of
April, Mr. Lincoln's reply in writing to the Committee
was "distinctly pacific and he expressly disclaimed all purpose of war." The next day, the Committee left for Richmond, and the same train that bore them took also Lincoln's requisition upon the Governors of the States for an
army of 75,000 men to subjugate the South! Now, here
is Lincoln giving personal assurance of "pacific" intentions – disclaiming expressly all purpose of war, on April
14th – when on April 6th, he had sent Governor Pickens
word that an attempt to provision Sumter would be made,
and on April 12th, the hostile Federal fleet of eleven ves-

sels, twenty-six guns, and 2,400 men were just outside the harbor and coming in! Did it require all those men and cannon to land the bread-stuffs for sixty-three soldiers, or were they sent to garrison and hold the fort against the city and State for whose *defense* it had been built and equipped?

CHAPTER FOUR
It Was a Great War
☆ ☆ ☆ ☆

A people has but one dangerous enemy, and that is
government – Saint Just, France, A.D., 1793

Careful and competent judges (one a Cabinet
member, Secretary Shaw, of the United States Treasury)
tell us that there were, during the four years, three thousand, one hundred and twenty, conflicts of arms! "The
total cost of the Civil War has been moderately estimated
at $8,000,000,000. In addition to which the Government
spent $800,000,000, mainly in war expenses, and large
outlays were made by States, whilst the property destroyed is beyond computation." (*Encyclopedia of United
States History*). "This estimate, Doctor Deering, is not
heavy enough, because it included an estimate of only
$1,500,000,000 for pensions. The official figures, which
I furnish, show that the pensions aggregated almost twice
that sum." If, then, we may trust this experienced and
very painstaking official in Washington, and if we add his
pension figures, we have the justly estimated cost of our
"late unpleasantness" – NINE AND A HALF BILLIONS.
Now, since nobody can comprehend such a sum – let it
pass! The money is gone anyway!

In the area that it overspread, in the populations it embraced, in the men it enlisted, in the money it cost, in the battles that were fought, in the lives that it sacrificed, in the questions that it settled, in the problems that it created, in the burdens that it imposed upon the black man, in the emancipation that it brought to the Southern white people, in the misery and poverty into which it plunged millions, in the wealth that it bestowed upon a favored few, in the antagonisms that it left for us and our children, it has earned a title to its greatness that will never be disputed while sun and moon endure! A single item of its expense remains and recurs, from year to year, as a reminder of what no man can ever fully understand, namely $145,937,000 – the present *yearly outlay for pensions, of one side only,* and that *after forty-two years* have passed away. The total expenditure for pensions alone has reached the enormous sum of $3,545,377,806.60, and no seer can see the end! This sum is more by $258,527,243.60 than was the cost of both the Army and Navy during the whole conflict. Yet legislation in this direction seems scarce begun. There were added to the rolls of pensioners last year – 34,974 names; and this year, under the "Service Pension Law," just enacted, it is estimated that 100,000 more people will be cared for by "the best Government that the world ever saw." The Government's estimate of this increase *annually* is $10,414,400.

There are now, forty-two years after the war's close, 666,345 soldier's names on the pension rolls. This is a longer line than the South had in all the years of the war. If the United States had bought and set free all the slaves on the American continent, and in Africa, and the islands of the sea, and had never shot a gun, or dug a grave, or builded a prison, or broken a heart, or pillaged a city, or burned a home, or laid waste an acre, how tremendous the saving would have been! Think! The estimated value, at the outbreak of the war, of all the slaves held in all our territory was only $2,000,000,000, and to free them, without law, we came out of the struggle with a debt, on August 31st, 1865, according to the Government bookkeeper's report, of $2,845,907,626.56 – so that, it is clear, we might have bought and freed every slave, paid the bill in cash, and had left a balance of $845,907,626.56. That would have been a mountain of money, not to speak of the brains, blood, hearts, homes, lives, labors, energies, materials, and everything else saved! Verily, the war wasn't a very economical transaction!

One general, who commanded in one march, through two or three States, confessed that his spoils and conflagrations "amounted to $100,000,000. Of this, $20,000,000 inured to our benefit, and the rest was mere waste and destruction" – so said Sherman. That was in Georgia and the Carolinas. Poor Virginia, Mother of States and of Statesmen, no man has ever had the courage to count up thy costs. In one of thy valleys, seventy mills full of grain, with 2,000 barns containing farming implements, were fired to furnish light for the retreating invaders! It is no wonder that the cruel commander could report to his superior, *"The next crow that flies over the Valley must carry his own rations."* The marvel is that, any American commander could be so savage, so utterly heartless, as to authorize such destruction! That Sherman left a swath of blight and fire, and ruins and bones, from forty to sixty miles wide, and reaching through three broad commonwealths makes us marvel at man's inhumanity to man! In its wicked and awful rage, Sherman's army was more cruel than fire, or famine or plague – for fire spared people; famine spared property; plague spared both food and property; that army spared nothing; it left a desert without an oasis and almost without life. And besides Sherman's, there were Sheridan's and Hunter's ravages, as fearful as fire could make them! Enough, the story is unbearable! General Bradley Johnson says, "The face of the country was so changed that one born in it could scarcely recognize it."

It was a wicked and cruel war, yet not wholly bad or fought in vain. It had a brighter side – THE SOUTH-ERN SIDE. Lee's address to his advancing army at Chambersburg, Pennsylvania, made the statement that "civilization and Christianity would not allow retaliation upon enemies. It must be remembered that we make war only upon armed men, and that we cannot take vengeance for the wrongs our people have suffered, without lower-ing ourselves in the eyes of all whose abhorrence has been excited by the atrocities of our enemies, and offending against Him to whom vengeance belongeth, without whose favor and support, our efforts must all prove in vain." We are given the effect of this order by Mr. Charles F. Adams, of Boston, in his New York address, January 26th, 1903. "In scope and spirit Lee's order was observed, and I doubt if a hostile force ever advanced in an enemy's country, or fell back from it in retreat, leaving behind it less cause for hate and bitterness than did the Army of Northern Virginia." Remembering that this gen-tleman was an officer in the army of General Grant, we could hardly wish for a better witness. But he speaks the bare truth, nothing more. A Union citizen who lived in Danville, Kentucky, when Bragg's army passed through it, told me that his soldiers did not take the apples ripe in his orchard. It is said that Bragg had some soldiers shot for stealing chickens. My captain made me return to a prisoner his old hat; wouldn't allow the swap; and he once ordered me to ride my horse "until he falls," rather than "press" one on the march to risk being captured rather than swap a tired horse for a fresh one! Such was the spirit and discipline of the Southern soldiers.

And the war had its compensations. It wrought in us, and for us, some things that nothing else could. It made us a better and a greater people; it brought men nearer to God, and made women more like Christ; it showed human nature at its best, and grace in her divinest form. Faith worked by love, and the faith we had in God, and Joe Johnston, and the Army of Northern Virginia, knew no bounds. Hope was never so heavenly. We realized the truth – "A man's life consisteth not in the abundance of the things which he possesseth." We *had* little to eat, and less to drink, and nearly nothing to wear, but what we *were going to have* "when this cruel war is over" would have satisfied King Croesus himself! Charity never failed us, patience had her perfect work; self-denial was glorified before our very eyes. The spirit of sympathy and helpfulness spread over the land. Every man was his "brother's keeper." Most things were done or endured for the public good. We "had all things common" – except tea and coffee, of which there wasn't enough to be divided. Tobacco and toilet soap were about the only things a man might not beg, borrow or steal. We were at our best and approximated the Christ life. We lived and moved and had our being for Dixie and Independence. The fires of patriotism never burned more intensely in Revolutionary times, or on Grecian altars. We forgot the fashions, threw away useless purses and grew rich in noble examples and self-sacrificing deeds. We came home worn and weary, hungry and ragged, broken in health and bankrupt in everything, but we gave the world our Lee and Davis, and the mighty "Stonewall," with the Hills, and Johnstons, and Helm, and Hanson, and Stuart, and Forrest, and Morgan, and Breckinridge, and Admiral Semmes, and Private Sam Davis, the "Boy Martyr" of Tennessee! No money could buy these immortal names; no historic doubts can blacken them or cause us to forget. The war made us a solid South, a self-reliant, self-respecting people. We stand together, and will stand in the face of creation, and we feel "the satisfaction that proceeds from the consciousness of duty faithfully performed." For myself, I would not barter that for all Kentucky! I have been ashamed of many things in my life, but the recollection of my course as a Confederate soldier has been for forty years, my chief joy and pride! If ever I was fit to live or willing to die, if ever I was worthy of my father's name or my mother's blood, if ever I was pleased with my place, suited to my rank, or satisfied with my sinful self – it must have been whilst I was marching under that white-starred cross upon that blood-red banner against the invaders of my native Southland. For that I want no forgiveness in this world or the next. I can adopt the saying of my great Commander, General Lee: "If all were to be done over again, I should act in precisely the same manner; I could have taken no other course without dishonor."

CHAPTER FIVE
It Was a Hopeless War

The greatest friend of truth is time: her greatest enemy is
prejudice, and her constant companion is humility. – Charles
Caleb Colton, *Lacon*, 1820, A.D.

General Lee said to General Pendleton, a day or
two before the surrender, –

> I never believed that we could, against the gi-
> gantic combination for our subjugation, make good in
> the long run our Independence, unless foreign powers
> should directly or indirectly assist us. But such consider-
> ations really made with me no difference. If all were to
> be done over again, I should act in precisely the same
> manner. I could have taken no other course without dis-
> honor.

Comrades, how could 650,000 town-men and
country boys contend successfully against 2,987,776 Federal soldiers and sailors – an host containing 2,128,304
men more than Dixie ever enlisted? Lacking only 12,224,
it was a mass of 3,000,000 men. Yet it took more than
four and a quarter Yankee soldiers four full years to whip

each Confederate! It was 7,652,335 Southern people
against 23,785,722 Northern, with our 4,000,000 slaves
in the rear to plot and spy, to deceive, distract and devour
us. And this estimate must be reduced by 3,000,000
Unionists of the Border States. It was these things that
made us desperate.

The war was hopeless also for lack of ships, and
by reason of the blockade that shut out every resource
from abroad. It was hopeless for lack of rail transportation, which let our food rot in piles in Georgia, while
Lee's legions were starving in the trenches in Virginia.
Our Commander-in-Chief allowed himself "but two small
rations of meat a week." No bread or bacon at Amelia
Court House compelled the surrender at Appomattox. It
was hopeless for lack of arms. At Manassas, a John
Brown pike was handed out instead of a Mauser rifle.
When at McMinnville, I asked General Morgan for arms,
he pointed to the Yankee camp and bade me help myself.
For horse, I rode a sore-back, broken-down "plug;" for
bridle, I had a halter; for saddle, a naked "tree;" for stir-
rups, a loop of rope; and I went into my first fight with a
single cartridge and some mental reservation.

It was hopeless through Grant's refusal to exchange prisoners; a refusal made through General B. F.
Butler to General Lee's proposal of exchange, "with a
view of alleviating the sufferings of our soldiers" – made
for General Grant, to whom, of course, it was submitted
– a refusal made by the most offensive man and in the
most offensive form possible, in the shape of an argument
by Butler to obtain recognition of negro equality for some
colored soldiers captured and confined by the Confederates. This subject was introduced and shrewdly handled
with the intention of insulting the Southern Commander

and his soldiers, so as to preclude all possibility of an exchange of white prisoners. That such was its design, Butler confessed before a Congressional committee, in his official report, and he testifies "that it was for the purpose of carrying out the wishes of the Lieutenant-General commanding that no prisoners of war should be exchanged."

Commissioner Ould, after several conferences with Butler over the matter, says, "We had reached what we both thought a tolerably satisfactory basis." But when Grant came the next day, he gave Butler "the most emphatic verbal directions not to take any step by which another able-bodied man should be exchanged until further orders from him." In his official report, Butler says, "I wrote an argument showing our right to our colored soldiers. This argument set forth our claims in the most offensive form possible, consistently with ordinary courtesy of language." The scheme succeeded. Lee declined to exchange, except "upon the basis established by the cartel." This never had contained any recognition of *runaway slaves* as soldiers.

When afterwards General Lee called on President Davis to tell him the result of his attempt, and had, says Mr. Davis, listened to the expression of my bitter disappointment, he said – "We have done everything in our power to mitigate the suffering of prisoners and there is no just cause of further responsibility on our part."

In a dispatch to Butler, Grant tries to justify his refusal by saying, –

> On the subject of exchange, I differ from General Hitchcock. It is hard on our men held in Southern prisons not to exchange them, but it is humanity to those left in the ranks, to fight our battles. Every man, released on parole or otherwise, becomes an active soldier

against us at once, either directly or indirectly. If we commence a system of exchange, which liberates all prisoners taken, we will have to fight on until the whole South is exterminated. If we hold those caught, they amount to no more than dead men. At this particular time, to release all prisoners North would insure Sherman's defeat, and would compromise our safety here.

This humiliating official confession is dated, "City Point, August 18, 1864."

Another effort made by the Confederate Government was to obtain the exchange of "officer for officer, and man for man," regardless of *"the excess,"* which the cartel contemplated and comprehended. This offer was not noticed at all, although it would have turned loose every Yankee in our prisons! The next proposal made by the Southern side was to send the United States authorities "their sick and wounded without requiring any equivalents." This was but partially carried out, because, although attempted in the summer, the enemy sent no transportation for their poor diseased soldiers until November, when our people, unable to move the sick and wounded from distant places, "substituted 5,000 well men." In return, about 3,000 of our wounded boys were sent to us, the other 500 who started having died on the journey. For sound men the enemy would willingly have given us those dying ones.

It should be remembered also that in consequence of the sickness and suffering among the Yankee prisoners, owing to confinement, climate, scarcity of good food, and lack of proper medicines, our Commissioner, Mr. Ould, offered to buy with gold, cotton or tobacco, the needed drugs from the Federal authorities, "at even two or three prices, if required," and assured them that the medicines would be used "exclusively for the treatment of Union prisoners." He also agreed, if it were desired, that such remedies might be brought to, and distributed among the sufferers by United States' surgeons. President Davis says, – "Incredible as it may appear, it is nevertheless, strictly true that no reply was ever received to this offer."

Mercy might well have given up with such a repulse, but one more heroic attempt was put forth. Mr. Davis sent from the prisoners at Andersonville a delegation of four men to Washington to try, if their personal presence and pleading could soften the official heart, and set the captives free. Mr. Lincoln wouldn't even see them, and they returned, as they had promised, to confinement. There is in Richmond, on file, among the papers of the Southern Historical Society, a letter from the wife of the chairman of that delegation (he is now dead), in which she says that her husband always said that "he was more contemptuously treated by Secretary of War Stanton, than he ever was at Andersonville."

The refusal of the Federal Government to exchange prisoners was at first based upon its unwillingness to recognize as a belligerent power the Confederate States. In 1861, General Grant wrote to General Leonidas Polk, who sought of him an exchange – "I recognize no 'Southern Confederacy' my self, but will communicate with higher authorities for their views." These "views" agreed with Grant's. When on July 2, 1863, Mr. Alexander H. Stephens was sent by President Davis on an errand of mercy to Washington to treat for the release of all prisoners, he was turned back from Fortress Monroe, and his Government scorned as "insurgent," his request was declared "inadmissible." A "mission of simple humanity" inadmissible! Tell it not in Gath!

When *"the excess"* of captives was in Confederate hands, exchanges and paroles were mutual and easy. The trouble began when the tide turned, and the surrenders at Donaldson and Vicksburg had given the excess to the Northern side. To have exchanged them then would have strengthened us the most.

Toward the end of the struggle, all excuses and pretenses were boldly cast away and the policy of destroying us by *"depletion"* (Grant's word) openly admitted. All Southern prisoners must be held and starved and shot to death; this land must be laid waste, its stores and crops consumed, its homes robbed and burned, its people, old and young, driven into the woods, its flocks and herds devoured or carried off, and even its farming implements and granaries given to the flames, so that the coming years must be years of famine to such as might outlive the battle and hospital and prison and deportation! We had had "war to the knife, and knife to the hilt," as among savages, but it was too merciful! War must henceforth be waged against helpless captives, innocent children and our defenseless women. Their food and shelter and all that might make life tolerable must be taken away! In three pregnant sentences Major-General B. F. Butler avows the policy and fastens the responsibility of it on the Federal Government. He writes:

> I have felt it my duty to give an account with this particular carefulness of my participation in the business of exchange of prisoners, the orders under which I acted, and the negotiations attempted, which comprise a faithful narration of all that was done, so that all may become a matter of history. The great importance of the questions; the fearful responsibility for

the many thousands of lives which, by the refusal to exchange, were sacrificed by the most cruel forms of death, from cold, starvation, and pestilence of the prison pens in Raleigh and Andersonville, being more than all the British soldiers killed in the wars of Napoleon; the anxiety of fathers, brothers, sisters, mothers, wives, to know the exigency which caused this terrible, and perhaps, as it may seem to them, useless and unnecessary destruction of those dear to them, by horrible deaths, each and all have compelled me to this exposition, so that it may be seen that those lives were spent as a part of the system of attack upon the rebellion, devised by the wisdom of the General-in-Chief of the armies, to destroy it by depletion, depending upon our superior numbers to win the victory at last. The loyal mourners will doubtless derive solace from this fact, and appreciate all the more highly the genius which conceived the plan, and the success won at so great a cost.

The "loyal mourners" will never forgive General Grant, in my opinion.

No wonder that poor Wirz was hung! Somebody had to die! A scape-goat was never needed more. Unhappy Soul! to be the vicarious victim of one's friends would be hard enough, but to have to die for the sins of one's enemies – who can describe that anguish? Of this judicial murder, Alexander H. Stephens, Vice-President, says: –

The efforts which have been so industriously made to fix the odium of cruelty and barbarity on Mr. Davis and other high officials under the Confederate Government, in the matter of prisoners, in the face of all the facts, constitute one of the bloodiest attempted outrages upon the truth of history which has been essayed;

not less than the infamous attempt to fix upon him and other high officials on the Confederate side, the guilt of Mr. Lincoln's assassination. Whatever unnecessary privations and sufferings prisoners on both sides were subjected to, the responsibility rested not upon Mr. Davis or the Confederate authorities. It was the fault of the Federal authorities in not agreeing to and carrying out an immediate exchange, which Mr. Davis was at all times anxious to do. The men at the head of affairs at Washington were solely responsible for all these sufferings. Neither Libby nor Belle Isle, nor Salisbury nor Andersonville, would have had a groaning prisoner of war but for the refusal of the Federal authorities to comply with the earnest desire of the Richmond Government for an immediate exchange upon the most liberal and humane principles.

As to the *treatment of prisoners* in our hands, Mr. Stephens is just as clear and strong. He declares that they shared equally with the Confederate soldiers whatever there was to be had. I myself happen to know that in Georgia the produce of "the tax in kind" stored in Government warehouses was divided into equal parts, and one part sent to the Confederate soldiers and the other part to the Yankee prisoner, at Andersonville. They had what we had – share and share alike. When told by his Commissary General that the supplies were so short that rations for either the Confederate soldier or Yankee prisoners must be reduced; Lee said, "While I have no authority in the case, my desire is that the prisoners shall have equal rations with my men." There is, however, no use to quote any man, when we have official returns of the United States Surgeon General Barnes showing that a much greater number of Confederates died in Northern prisons than of Federals in Southern stockades; and this in spite of the fact that we held 50,000 more Federals in captivity than the Yankee had of our soldiers. In round numbers they had only 220,000 Confederates; we held 270,000 Federals. Of these only 22,576 died on our hands; whilst, of the 220,000 men held in Northern prisons, 26,436 died. In other words, with about 50,000 more prisoners to feed and guard we had a loss of nearly 4,000 less than the Union people lost of our men. "The per cent, of Federal deaths was under *nine* in Southern prisons: the per cent. of Confederate deaths in Yankee prisons was *over twelve.*" And that, too with the markets of the world open to them for all needed supplies, and their bank-vaults full to overflowing with gold and greenbacks with which to purchase! Query; If in our *poverty,* we saved three per cent. more lives than they, what per cent. might they have saved through their *wealth, if they had been willing?*

Repeated efforts have been made to disprove, or somehow dispose of, these official figures of Surgeon General Barnes. They are so convincing and cruelly condemnatory that they cannot be endured. Unfortunately for our friends, the enemy, their shame and the attempt to hide it came all too late. The report of Dr. Barnes is quoted by Vice-President A. H. Stevens, in his great volume, *The War Between the States.* And it has editorial mention in *The National Intelligencer* of Washington, June 2, 1869. No such report can *now* be found! Nor is any knowledge of its existence admitted by any Department of the Government. Its disappearance is a mystery, but one not so hard to explain as the frequent reference to it by Southern orators who couldn't have seen what never existed. And the failure of Northern speakers and writers to deny its damaging showing for many years is even more a mystery. When Ben Hill quoted it in 1876 in U.S. Senate, why was it not questioned? *Why?*

The war was hopeless for want of revenue, credit and a sound currency; for want of mines and manu-factories; for lack of sailors and ships of war with which to keep open our ports and closed our river-gates, and for lack of almost all that enters into the business of aggressive warfare. It was hopeless for want of materials, of skilled mechanics, suitable shops, blankets, clothing, shoes, medicines, salt, lead, iron, copper, leather, sulphur, saltpetre and anesthetics. I have seen trains loaded with ammunition and soldiers stopped for want of axle grease. We fought hunger and sickness, cold and nakedness. On the Rapidan, Lee had a thousand men without a blanket and 3,000 hatless, barefooted fellows in the snow at one time; but we tightened our belts, gritted our teeth, and held on to hope. The last charge at Appomattox was as gallant as the first at Manassas. We had pride and patriotism to spare, but we couldn't feed the living, or raise again our dead! – And so, *we failed!* We sank in sorrow and sheer exhaustion, but not in shame. General Stephen D. Lee says: "We fought until about half of our enlisted strength was under the sod." And this enlisted strength was not near so great as many have imagined. Charles A. Dana, the Assistant Secretary of War, says, in the *American Cyclopedia* (1875): – "The Adjutant-General S. Cooper of C. S. Army estimates the entire available Confederate forces capable of active services in the field was 600,000 men, and not more than 400,000 were enrolled at any one time. The Confederate States never had in the field at once more than 200,000 men." (See Volume V, page 232.) Here we rest our Cause!

Boys, you loved it well, and stood by it to the

end! God bless you for it! You will receive to-night, from the fair hands of our Confederate women, the bronze CROSS OF HONOR. It will perish, but not the sweet satisfaction of having done your duty, nor the blessed consciousness of having been in the right! Good-night, Comrades, good-night!

Heroic deeds are deathless; and they live
Unmarred whilst empires crumble into dust,
They master fame, and life and glory give
To storied urn and animated bust.

SOURCES

☆ ☆ ☆ ☆

General Lee, by Fitzhugh Lee, his nephew and cavalry commander.

Robert E. Lee and the Southern Confederacy, by Henry A. White, M.A., D.D., Ph. D.

Recollections and Letters of R. E. Lee, by Robert E. Lee, Jr.

Personal Reminiscences of General R. E. Lee, by Rev. Dr. J. Wm. Jones, Chaplain A.N.Va.

Genesis of the Civil War, by Major-General S.W. Crawford, U.S.A.

Rise and Fall of the Confederate Government, by Jefferson Davis.

Is Davis a Traitor? by Albert Taylor Bledsoe, A.M., LL.D., late a Professor of the University of Virginia.

The Southern States of the American Union, by J.L.M. Curry, LL.D., etc.

A View of the Constitution of the United States of America, by Wm. Rawle, LL.D., Philadelphia, 1825.

The True History of the Civil War, by Guy Carleton Lee, Ph.D., of the Johns Hopkins University.

Service Afloat, by Admiral Raphael Semmes, of the Confederate States Navy.

A School History of the United States, by Susan Pendleton Lee.

Confederate Veteran, Official Organ of the U.C.V.; Sons of U.C.V.; Daughters of the Confederacy; by S.A. Cunningham,, late of Army of Tennessee," Nashville, Tenn., A.D. 1892–1907. This able, beautiful and invaluable magazine may be seen in ten thousand Southern homes, where it enjoys the preference and deserves the honor of all Dixie's defenders over its periodical rivals. The *first* of its class, and the *best!*

Made in the USA
Charleston, SC
30 September 2016